Plant Layout

and Facility Planning

Edition 2

Other industrial engineering books by Jack Greene, 2013
See Amazon's CreateSpace

Industrial Engineering: Theory, Practice & Application
Business and Production Management, Productivity and Capacity
ISBN-13: 978-1482301793
(Also in a Kindle edition)

Time and Motion Study
For Capacity and Productivity. 978-1492221425
ISBN-13: 978-1492221425
 (Also in a Kindle edition)

Cost Reduction
In Business Management
ISBN-13: 978-1492261100
 (Also in a Kindle edition)

Replaced by this book, published in 2011

Plant Design, Facility Layout, Floor Planning

Facility Relocation, Merger, and Consolidation:
Another commercial facility, in addition to or instead of?

Plant Layout

and Facility Planning

Edition 2

By Jack Greene

ISBN-13:   978-1491222393
ISBN-10:   1491222395

Preface, Plant Layout and Facility Planning, Edition 2

Layout, or the physical organization of people, materials and machines within a workplace, is at the very heart of productivity. This book will enable creation of new productive layouts quickly and smoothly.

Plant layout and facility planning are closely associated in industrial and commercial enterprises, and affect operating efficiency and productivity now and in the future.

Layout chapters focus on product flow, space utilization, and functional relationships; facility planning chapters address strategy for and how to achieve relocation, growth, consolidation, site search, a campus.

Chapters explain what and why, and list actions to create productive layouts quickly and smoothly within the physical constraints of the facility. They improve project management by highlighting which practices to utilize and which missteps to avoid, and extend the technical capabilities of your staff.

◆ ◆ ◆

This book will guide your organization through practical strategic and hands-on instruction, enable creation of new productive layouts quickly and smoothly within the physical constraints of the facility, as well as

- Consider and optimize factors which extend the layout's contribution now and through the years.

- Extend the technical capabilities of your staff .

- Improve project management by highlighting which practices to utilize and which missteps to avoid.

Facility layouts and floor plans tend to be replaced infrequently, because a revision can be expensive and cause disruption as it is installed. But a thoughtful layout can achieve many efficiencies in a new or existing facility.

In practice the elements of plant layout and of facility planning are likely to be required in any order; the specific tool or technique will depend on your particular project.

◆ ◆ ◆

The author, plant layout and facility planning

Jack Greene has headed division or corporate industrial engineering for three Fortune 250 companies; ITT, Abbott Labs, and Bausch & Lomb.

Adept in all aspects of facility planning, Jack Greene has successfully completed layout and facility planning projects for manufacturing, distribution center, R&D, and administration operations in more than forty operations.

The projects have involved simple layout of existing operations, and much more complex existing and new facilities; to attain objectives for capacity increase, site search, acquisition, relocation, consolidation, expansion; in the US and internationally, for manufacturing companies both large (FORTUNE 250) and small

His expertise in cost effective manufacturing and management practices extends through the semiconductor, pharmaceutical, optical, steel, lighting, electronic assembly, canning, recreational, consumer products, hospitality, construction and communication industries. He has frequently represented manufacturing and facility interests within due diligence and feasibility studies for merger, acquisition and consolidation projects.

Jack founded Jackson Productivity Research Inc. in 1991. Emphasizing individual, boutique attention, JPR provides on-site services as well as remote assistance to clients via phone and email.

◆ ◆ ◆

Thanks for the purchase, I hope the information proves to be useful. Let me know.

Good luck.

Jack Greene
Jackson Productivity Research Inc.
http://jacksonproductivity.com
Email jack@jacksonproductivity.com

◆ ◆ ◆

Table of Contents

♦ ♦ ♦

Layout Examples

See http://jacksonproductivity.com.draw.pdf for a couple dozen thought-provoking layout templates, examples of plant layout and design within particular building types. On line they are easier to read and print out than in a book, and I can add to them.

♦ ♦ ♦

Section on Plant Layout, Facility Design, Floor Planning

This section will guide your organization through practical strategic and hands-on instruction, enable creation of new productive layouts quickly and smoothly within the physical constraints of the facility, as well as

- Consider and optimize factors which extend the layout's contribution now and through the years.

- Extend the technical capabilities of your staff .

- Improve project management by highlighting which practices to utilize and which missteps to avoid.

Facility layouts and floor plans tend to be replaced infrequently, because a revision can be expensive and cause disruption as it is installed. But a thoughtful layout can achieve many efficiencies in a new or existing facility.

Oh yes. If you want a universal template or layout or formula, this section won't help much. I'm sorry but there is no single quick fix, because equipment, process, flow, and building plans have such a major effect on layout and they vary widely. Twenty six layout examples are referenced on line however which offer guidance, but the variable factors in your facility will be unique, so your layout will be unique. This section will assist you to create that unique, cost-effective layout.

◆ ◆ ◆

Chapter 1   Layout benefits and concepts

Layout, or the physical organization of people, materials and machines within a workplace, is at the very heart of productivity and industrial engineering.

A. Benefits of a thoughtful layout

By analyzing and improving workplace (and workspace) layout, it is possible to:
1. Position equipment, process, materials and personnel efficiently within the facility, existing or new.

2. Organize and cut through the "spaghetti" flow that adds distance and confusion. Optimize product flow through the process, make it visible. Simplify and reduce product and personnel movement.

3. Place work stations and inventory to amplify their interactions.

4. Add output, capacity and utilization by relieving space constraints.

5. Reduce handling and damage to product.

6. Simplify organization of material from receiving through shipping.

7. Allow for future growth or consolidation.

When your organization makes improvements, you can achieve immediate results, as well as form a base for continuing improvement.

◆ ◆ ◆

B. There is no universal layout template because one solution does not fit all

If you want a universal template or layout or formula, this book won't help much. I'm sorry but there is no single quick fix, because equipment, process, flow, and building plans have such a major effect on layout and they vary widely. You will have to apply layout principles to your unique situation, objectives, timeline, and budget.

Twenty five layout examples are included in the last section and they offer a demonstration of good layout practice in different situations. Your layout will be unique however, because the variable factors in your facility will be unique. This book will assist you to apply principles and create that unique, cost-effective layout.

Layout requires fitting workstations into a building floor plan but that step usually is a later one. First define the operating characteristics of your process, flow and routing of output; equipment size, capability and capacity considering product mix; crew sizes and skills; inventory and cycle time goals; material handling and safety. Recognize characteristics and dimensions of the building, and you will find a new layout will be much easier to plan, and more effective when implemented.

A new layout will require work and thought and later, cost to implement. Benefits can pay back the investment, and perhaps this book will improve the return in your situation.

◆ ◆ ◆

C. If not a universal template, then what?

A new layout can be achieved quickly even if it is not a universal, off the shelf, template. As with any other project, experience and skill can produce rapid and effective results.

A layout can be large or small in scope, tailored to your objectives, timetable and budget. Major layouts often are phased over time. Remember it may years before you perform the next re-layout; better get this one right.

Plan and implement a layout with your own resources, or those of an experienced consultant such as Jackson Productivity Research Inc. Develop layouts to meet operating criteria and schedules, relieve constraints, cut operating costs, simplify flow, add capacity or require less space, bring together different or new processes and equipment, allow for future growth.

◆ ◆ ◆

D. Key steps to achieve successful layouts

1. Primary reasons for creating a layout are a) to generate a better flow pattern for materials and / or people in an existing area, or b) to set up a new or different facility.

2. In either case, it is important first to define the physical characteristics of the space;

11

dimensions, major access points, building limitations including floor loads and ceiling heights, regulations affecting the space, rest rooms, fire codes and emergency routes. Then, plot several options as "block" layouts, discuss them with the stakeholders, and choose an efficient, safe, long lasting arrangement with good flow. Finally, "detail" the block layout down to the level necessary to install equipment, furnishings, utilities and connections.

3. The type of inventory system in use is also a major factor early in a manufacturing layout. Will material be supplied Just in Case, the traditional Materials Requirement Planning technique, or will the focus be on a lean process, or Just In Time delivery? Layout principles will fit either system, but a layout designed for JIT won't generally provide enough storage space for Just in Case; a JIC layout will generally be too spacious for JIT. Know what system you will use, in order to assign the correct amount of space to materials, in the appropriate places.

4. A good flow pattern for materials and people within the physical geometry of your equipment and facilities should be a driving force for any layout. It may not be possible to quantify all the benefits, but many productive practices follow from a careful layout; materials movement without retracing steps, visibility of inventory and of work, easy access of direct and support people, superior material handling, safety, housekeeping, emergency routes.

5. A classic method to gain room is to move into what is currently storage space, warehouses for instance. That often can be a practical option, especially if a concurrent objective is to reduce inventory. As a caution, warehouse ceiling height and solid floor may not fit manufacturing preferences very well.

6. A prerequisite to a layout is to define material handling into an area, considering material dimensions and weight, elevation changes, trucks, conveyors, etc. Also determine how utilities will be provided; while overhead supply is often easier than under-floor it may block access to equipment and interfere with sight lines and vision.

7. A recent client believed that his current layout did not reflect management's desire for employees to enjoy their working environment, and we created much less cluttered, more safe, conditions with a layout. He also wanted to be able to show off the highly capable modern equipment to his potential customers; that is possible today.

◆ ◆ ◆

E. Layout implementation

Layouts tend to be fixed in place for a long time, because a new one can be expensive and cause disruption as it is installed. And too, a layout will probably be obsolescent soon after it is put in, due to new equipment or product or a shift in volumes. There is no magic solution to this dilemma, unless your crystal ball is clearer than mine. If possible, try to create "pockets" of empty floor space in the layout, with nothing physically installed there. Then when a new requirement arises, you will have room to maneuver.

It is difficult to play a "checkers" game, to move sequentially from place to place, if there is no empty space on your checkerboard to start with.

Layout implementation cost and complexity varies; to avoid production interruption for instance, or if utilities such as water and drains are under a concrete floor, a change will be long and expensive. Many modern buildings provide utility access from the ceilings, even drains, and changes can be accomplished much more readily and swiftly. If possible, place really permanent objects together to minimize the obstructions to later expansion or rearrangement.

◆ ◆ ◆

F. A building addition

When a new area is to be laid out and built, be sure to address not only the immediate need but also the future as well as it can be anticipated, to keep the layout effective for some time. If the budget allows, build in extra space to provide options for future actions. Be sure to plan where a major expansion will be even if it is not built until later. Then in the layout do not block later access to the expansion route with permanent facilities such as docks, rest rooms, steam generators, water treatment equipment, chemical processes, waste treatment.

Plan the building layout before setting the final design for the facility if possible, because existing walls and access points restrict flow and placement of equipment.

◆ ◆ ◆

Chapter 2   Layout and how it can enhance productivity

A. Layout objectives are to enhance productivity

1. A successful facility layout will meet basic objectives:
   - Match today's business mission to the facility.

   - Fit it all in; equipment, processes and people.

   - Arrange process, equipment and material to perform operations efficiently and safely.

   - Minimize space-related constraints.

2. The layout should also meet enhanced objectives, if possible:
   - Allow for future growth or consolidation.

   - Show off modern equipment to potential customers.

   - Minimize cost, maximize benefit.

◆ ◆ ◆

B. The business model and characteristics of a facility affect the final layout

Understand these factors and keep them in mind because they definitely affect the layout that will be most suitable. For instance, a JIT flow by definition will not have significant inventory space among the machines, and a cellular equipment grouping may well be favored with JIT.

1. What is the manufacturing model for the organization?
       Batch, job shop, make to stock

2. What fundamental inventory control process is followed?
       Just In Time, or Just in Case, or some of each to fit the product

3. How will equipment be grouped?
       Cell; necessary equipment grouped for a product or sequence, or
       Modular arrangement, all one type of equipment together

4. What is the charter for equipment?
   Dedicated to a product, or multipurpose

◆ ◆ ◆

C. Layout tools and techniques to gain efficiency

Utilize the following tools and techniques to create effective layout options. These actions are not ranked, as their importance will not be the same in all situations.

1. Rearrange facilities and equipment to create shorter flow paths. Organize and cut through the "spaghetti" flow that adds distance and confusion. Layout steps as a "straight line" flow, perhaps more accurately called "direct" flow because sometimes it must turn to accommodate building geometry between receiving and shipping docks. Reduce product movement first and personnel secondarily.

2. Place work stations and inventory to optimize interactions of material and information flow with associated stations, but not with dissimilar ones. Also consider negative features such as vibration, noise, heat and energy radiation, odor.

3. If there is space available to do so, assign unused floor sections throughout the process for future expansion. If a future action is already identified, dedicate a space for it.

4. Make product flow and inventory through the process visible.

5. Reduce non-value-added activity such as handling.

6. Plan comprehensively for movement of raw materials, in-process, and finished products throughout the operation including the handling system, aisle widths, and access to production equipment. Size storage areas according to the fundamental inventory control process in B. 2 above. Consider height when called for.

7. Improve floor space utilization through appropriately sized aisles, and equipment positioning, within building constraints.

8. Reserve high ceilings, and high load capacity floors, for equipment that requires them.

9. Place fixed equipment, for instance those with foundations or piping or air handling or waste treatment, so that it can remain in place at the time of a future expansion or re-layout. (Even if the resulting flow is not totally efficient.)

15

10. Correct building shortcomings at the time of a layout, because the next rearrangement may not occur for a time.

11. Consider the locations of plant connections to energy and utilities. Reduce the internal distribution network if possible, although product flow is usually a more important consideration.

◆ ◆ ◆

Chapter 3   Work flow and facility layout

Facility layout is not the first step, but a later action to take to position equipment, processes and people in a building. First create the right work flow, then the layout easily follows.

Your organization is different from others; products, equipment, processes, building shape, routing, inventory practice. Your work flow and subsequent layout will also be different.

Work flow starts with a combination of your own objectives, operating practices and geometry of the facility. But to these factors you will have to apply principles of productivity in order to create an effective flow and productive layout.

This article explains the components that will affect your flow, floor layout and facility design.

A. Objectives

A new layout may be needed to set up an added facility, or to adapt a facility already in operation. In both cases it is wise to plan carefully, because layouts tend to remain in place for years; better get this one right.

A layout will be planned for a given set of assumptions, and they should be carefully written and reviewed by all concerned. A production forecast will be a critical factor for instance, to anticipate both products and volumes expected. Your crystal ball should anticipate long term changes such as new products, new technology, changes in the economy. It is not necessary to detail how the layout will provide for those eventualities, nor even to build the space. But identify where a new addition should go if it is necessary in a few years' time; don't block access now to a later action. Create a physical path now for later actions.

Cost constraints for the project must be considered as well as the time frame and calendar. Layout revisions, in phases, are often planned over an extended time; first do this, later do that. Also define the extent to which production may be interrupted, and when.

Identify the internal resources who are capable of performing the work necessary, then judge whether they can perform their normal work and direct a layout simultaneously. The best project manager I ever knew was not able to run his operating entity to his usual high standards, and a project, at the same time; take care in expecting a high level of performance in both tasks. Consultants such as my company are able to focus on the project, letting the client run the business.

◆ ◆ ◆

B. Operating practices

Many of your operating practices will affect a layout. Perhaps the most significant is inventory control. Do you practice just in time, or just in case? MRP or ERP, or another system? Where do you keep inventory throughout your process, both production and support? Is inventory current or a pack rat's delight? What inventory level is desired after the move?

Computer hardware can be an issue in a relocation, both servers and points of use. Be sure to involve your own IT people and any vendors early in the project. Try to allow a parallel operation of IT systems to minimize risks.

Telecommunications are a related concern to IT, although usually a bit simpler. Again, run in parallel if possible rather than depend on a complete cutover from one system to another.

Will you attempt to change major operating practices at the same time that you make a layout change? Then you are braver than I. One at a time is more likely to succeed, and if there is a problem you will find the answer more easily.

◆ ◆ ◆

C. Geometry

Physical property characteristics will determine the final layout. Lot size, zoning, easements, covenants, drainage, access, parking; access from roads. Building dimensions; load bearing and partition walls; ceiling heights; floor loading; piping, drains, utilities supply; heat, ventilation, air conditioning requirements and availability; docks and materials access; stairs and elevators and ramps; personnel access; amenities such as rest rooms and food service; offices and other service areas; these are given factors in the current facility that will shape and limit any changes.

The process has an effect on layout as well. Equipment and fixtures and furniture take up a fixed amount of floor space. Materials handling and personnel movement, considering product and handling equipment, will dictate plant aisles.

Storage will use a significant amount of space, not only for product but also for the supply and support items kept in hand. There are many kinds of racks for storage, different square footage and different heights. Aisle requirements vary as well depending on the rack.

Support and administration will require space with a particular criteria such as air conditioning.

Some functions will be difficult to relocate. They include plating and chemical treatment, water treatment, equipment in pits or on reinforced foundations, drains in the floor, stairways, elevators, structural mezzanines, etc. Processes with any kind of hazardous emission require special attention. Be sure to recognize these. If possible place them at the perimeter of the structure, but do not block off a future expansion.

◆ ◆ ◆

D. Principles of productivity

To achieve a new layout, there must be an empty place on the floor to start. Usually a checkers game is possible, move one function to the empty space, the move something else, until you are through. The process may be longer, with temporary inefficiencies, but often a phased change can avoid long interruptions even while achieving a complex relocation.

Flow as a general rule should not look like a bowl of spaghetti. A U shaped flow is often favored, or straight line flow. Move from start to finish of a process directly without doubling back if possible, whether the process is an automobile assembly or order processing or paying a tax bill. Start with the router or whatever defines the work sequence, arrange the equipment so product moves sequentially and directly through the process.

Before you get too deeply into the layout, let me point out that a time of revision is a very good time to pull out of the unnecessary activity, the waste. The heart of the Toyota Production System is to eliminate waste, and what better time than just before a major shift in location.

An incisive place to start is a series of questions to define waste, or non-value added. Business Week in March 2009 posed this test:
a. Will a customer pay for this activity?

19

b. Will my service fail without this activity?
c. Will I go to jail if I eliminate this activity?

Answer "no" to all three, and the activity can essentially be defined as waste.

Pull the activities out of the elements to be included in the new layout. Put them aside if you must, in another location for final disposal later, but remove them from the new active layout.

Docks and doors are used to bring material in and out. Use one entry for receiving, another for shipping if possible; dedicate one to waste handling if there is significant waste. Docks for semis are higher than those for a low van, and both will be useful. Provide ramps to allow wheeled vehicles to move in and out, or work in the parking lot.

Equipment that is used for more than one product can be difficult to place so that all product through it moves on a straight line. Product mix may also be a complicating factor. If the equipment is expensive, the cost of extra material handling will be a small price to pay for the economy of scale to keep the equipment well utilized.

If there are functions difficult to locate efficiently, you may be more successful in layout if you first plan flow in and out of them, and later fit in actions that do not relate to them.

Consider early how incoming material will be staged and moved into the process, and how in process material will be handled. Plan for the most bulky and the most numerous first and then the flow of other material.

Consider pedestrian traffic and separate it if possible from vehicle traffic.

◆ ◆ ◆

Chapter 4   Sequence of actions

to create layouts and implement the subsequent relocation

Much more information on these subjects is provide later; this chapter describes the sequence, more or less in this order,

A. Prepare basic information

List all equipment and furnishings to be included in the layout. Rigorously confirm that the list is complete. Group as necessary into departments, or cells, or categories.

Measure and prepare templates of primary, ancillary and support and equipment, including the footprint, operator workplace, material handling, and access. Accumulate the components to create "block templates" for the functional groups of equipment as they will be operated. Add up the square feet required.

Make and print layouts of the facility as it is. Note that as-built drawings may be inaccurate; confirm the print. Be sure to mark walls and columns and doors and points of access. Enter fixed functions which occupy building space. Add up the space available.

Compare space required to the space available. Resolve differences.

Use bills of material and routing sheets for major products or families to establish process steps to be addressed by the equipment layout.

◆ ◆ ◆

B. Develop a Favored Block Layout

Arrange the block layout templates above; create multiple options to illustrate overall flow though the facility as well as spatial relationships between departments or functions. Include administration, support, communication, and IT groups and their equipment and furnishings.

Most layout options will have good features and bad, so that the final selection will likely require a choice, or tradeoff, or further modifications. With management guidance, choose the favored option, obtain approval and signoff.

◆ ◆ ◆

C. Expand the favored block layout into adequate detail to implement it

After financial justification of the project, create detailed layouts options so that the final arrangement can be placed in the facility. Using the favored block layouts as a guide, position all of the equipment and furnishings that constitute each block. Make layouts detailed enough for placement and connection of utilities. With management guidance, choose the favored final arrangements, approve and sign off. It may well be useful to repeat steps B and C, to utilize new information and insights.

♦ ♦ ♦

D. Prepare the destination

Modify the destination facilities as necessary, mark the specific locations of equipment and furnishings on the floor, run utility supply lines, install and test communications and IT gear. This step may well involve building modifications, and be advised that specs for facility change, bidding, permits and community approvals and project management of the modifications can extend the calendar.

♦ ♦ ♦

F. Prepare for one or more relocations

Bid out rig and move contracts. Assemble documentation and support gear for all equipment. Plan and build inventories necessary for the transition. Pack up.

♦ ♦ ♦

G. The move day(s)

Disconnect utilities. Rig and move equipment. Move support parts, fixtures, documentation, material handling. Move office functions. Unpack, connect utilities.

♦ ♦ ♦

Chapter 5   The big picture for a layout

The layout is seen as the centerpiece of these chapters, but it usually takes place in a larger context. A layout is only a means to an end, usually a move or start up. This chapter expands that view, why the layout is necessary and what determines timing.

All layout projects are different. Although fundamentals tend to remain constant, objectives, economics, operating characteristics and preferences are unique to each project.

The combination of a layout project with a strategic facility action, such as a new plant, or merger, or consolidation, is not unusual. Other causes may be much more minor, a shift in product mix or volume, to need to install new equipment or technology, a window of opportunity to take a business action, phasing out or in a product.

A. Set the scope for the overall objective

Consider these major steps
1. Justification
a. Financial justification, perhaps one or more

- A capacity increase is necessary.
- Flow patterns through the facility are confused, a plate of spaghetti.
- The current layout does not fit the demand for products or services at the present time or in the future.
- New products will be produced in the facility.
- Old equipment should be replaced by new.
- Safety is compromised by layout.

b. Intangible justification
- The environment is not pleasant for employees.
- Customer perception of the facility is poor.

c. Timing factors, a window of opportunity.
Slow season for business offers a window, a lease expires, a business opportunity arises. A series of phased changes is desired.

d. Show-stoppers
- What could have a major negative impact on the project?
- How minimize the possibility?
- Communication to recognize serious problems.

e. Decision
Management gives the go-ahead, fully or qualified; or turns it down.

2. Context of the project

A layout will take place within the context of several components and considerations.

a. Establish team
Leader, department reps, management contact. Set procedures for operation. Set a priority considering the organization's other commitments, publicize the ranking, stick to it.

b. Destination
A checker game, series of moves? A sequence of events. Purchase necessary?

c. Characteristics of destination to accommodate the action and layout
Building size and shape. Internal areas size, floor load, ceiling height, surface finishes, lights, HVAC, plumbing, waste disposal, telecommunications, docks, parking, security. Need for construction / rehabilitation.

d. Disposition of source
Further "checkerboard" moves, or vacate.

e. Funding
Internal or external

f. Interruption to business
None, or fixed amount, or parallel operations in multiple facilities.

g. Effect on employees
- Transfer; terminate; hire.
- Training necessary.
- Help with relocation?

h. Specific timing will be affected by
- Today's activity at destination.
- Customer seasonality; construction lead times; communications cutover.
- Elapsed time likely for move itself.
- Target move date
- Week or weekend move; availability of resources.

3. Other steps beside layout, in the project

Please note that the layout itself, although a key activity, is not all there is to a project. These major steps are involved, with possible components and considerations

a. Source

Is documentation sufficient to move? Are some risks involved, waste disposal perhaps?

b. Destination layout and advance preparation.

- Block layout, then detailed layout and approvals.
- Zoning and Permits
- External regulation, perhaps from FDA, USDA, particular industry
- Construction, rehabilitation, furnish, equip, wire, HVAC, plumb, connect.
- Advance installation of communications gear and wiring.
- Move-in path.

c. Use of resources for the actual move

Employee participation, outside vendors and services. Equipment used. Chain of command. Alert mechanism for problems. Security plan for the move day.

d. Supplier and service vendor notification? Customer notification?

Change address if another property is involved.

4. Move

These major steps are involved, with possible components and considerations

a. Communication plan and cutover

Phones, computer, internet, mail

b. Equipment move and install

Disconnect, move, reconnect, startup.

c. Inventory move and install

Relocate, place, set records

d. Documents move and put away

Sort, move, replace in order.

e. The move itself
All hands on deck.

f. Dispose of source
Clean up for next use, or disposition.

g. Temporary relocation if necessary.

◆ ◆ ◆

B. Schedule and timing for a layout project

Timing for a facility action to implement a new or changed layout will depend on your circumstance. Do you have to meet a deadline, for instance a lease expires or there is a short window to move at a low period of activity. Or is your action free of time constraints? If the first layout and move is only one of a series, you may want to build a comprehensive plan or take the moves one by one.

Timing will determine your sense of urgency and work assignments.

1. With a firm move date
What are the key dates? Are they set in concrete? Even if they are mandated without considering the tasks involved, build them into the plans to see if it is practical to meet them. Revise dates only after you have a grasp of the costs of achieving them and the consequences of revising them.

Start with a series of "To Do" lists. Assign responsibility for each task; you have to do this before setting a viable timetable because Mary Lou may have 24 hours of work and you've only allowed her 8 hours.

Manipulate the "to do" and assignments within the time allowed

Build a calendar of events. Typically there will be .
a. A general plan; make a layout, then move from here to there on January 13.

b. Several supporting plans; involving perhaps existing location, destination, the move itself, support contract services, customer service, computer and telephone.

Resist the temptation to mandate a schedule before you know at least generally what extra work will be required of your staff. If you have a smooth running operation, there will be about enough people for every-day work. But a relocation requires work outside the norm; that is going to mean a consultant, overtime for your staff or some days when regular work is suspended.

2. With a flexible move date
Follow the same steps, but build a bit of reserve time into the plan to deal with unexpected events. Take advantage of circumstances, for instance a slow season, or scheduled vacations.

3. Final timing
Set your project action dates. Inform all concerned whether the date is critical or a target, or else you may incur some avoidable costs.

Create a master calendar, starting with the move date. Consider upcoming holidays and vacations in the plans. Calculate other major dates from the move date. Critical dates might include, depending on the complexity of the plan,

- General coordinator named
- Department coordinators named
- Customer service is interrupted; start and stop dates.
- Destination layouts approved
- Take possession of destination
- General preparation starts at destination
- Final packing starts
- Computer off at source; computer on at destination
- Phones off at source; phones on at destination
- Moving truck appears at source, departs source, arrives at destination, departs.
- Unpack to get operation going starts; is done
- Operation is back to normal

Creating and updating plans will be a continuing activity until the day of the move.

4. Assumptions and corollaries
Will the business be open during normal hours during the move? Yes calls for a weekend move or a shutdown if a longer time is required.

Is there a "slow season" for your business that fits into your calendar?

5. Critical path

Critical Path Management is a formal scheduling tool. It and other project scheduling and management tools may be found by searching Google. In the following discussion, the words "critical path" are in small print and relate to the concept that in relocation and expansion, a few actions will routinely determine timing in most cases.

Is the business computer-dependent? Yes means that the computer relocation will be on the critical path.

Will some equipment not be moved because upgrades or replacements will be used at the destination? If so the new equipment availability may determine the timing.

Is the destination ready or will some preparation be necessary there? If so, and a 'Certificate of Occupancy", a COO or C of O, is required, it will determine the move-in date.

Contractors may affect the timing. Performance to schedule should be specifically covered in purchase orders or contracts, perhaps with early completion bonus or charges for late performance. Remember that a hundred contractor-days can be accomplished by a hundred men for a day or one man a hundred days. Same cost, vastly different timing. If a contractor is on the critical path, require a double shift operation. It should not be more expensive; might actually cost him less because he doesn't have to pay as much equipment rental fee. But only a larger contractor might have the manpower to work a two shift operation.

◆ ◆ ◆

Chapter 6   Factors to consider in a layout and relocation

A. Administration of the layout project and subsequent relocation

Generally speaking, a project will be most successful when

- An overall project manager is named, reporting to management, with frequent access to management
- Individuals from the departments affected are named to represent their interests
- Good communications keep all informed, or even over-informed
- A clear overall objective is stated and monitored, with a time line and a budget
- A detailed action list is generated and monitored, with dates and responsibilities

◆ ◆ ◆

B. Destination detail

Perhaps the most important early step is to define the scope that is intended for the destination facility after the project is completed. Do this to state the underlying assumptions and elements of operation. It is very important that management complete this definition carefully, so that it can become the primary guidance for the implementation teams to locate, plan, acquire and startup the facility to meet management objectives.

This analysis does not address the detail of construction if it is required, either new or retrofit. Successful construction demands the same type of planning, administration, and follow-up that relocation does. The final step in construction is called a 'Certificate of Occupancy", a COO or C of O, permission from the code inspectors to move in. It can determine the move-in date. Be advised that the COO is often delayed, sometimes for reasons that do not seem logical or appropriate. Give the COO a great deal of attention so that your move in will not be delayed.

◆ ◆ ◆

C. Computer Changes

Will you replace or upgrade computer hardware or software at the time of the move? If so, you are a braver leader than I am. My suggestion is to change one thing at a time.

Computer changes in my experience require a period of parallel performance; operate both old and new systems at the same time and reconcile the differences. If it is possible to conduct a parallel path change in conjunction with a relocation or expansion or merger, do so. For instance install the new operation at the destination in advance of the move, and while the first system is still functioning. Otherwise perform the computer change in advance of the facility move, or following it.

Wiring for the computer operation at the destination may take a substantial period of time. Plan carefully because this move may be the best opportunity to create an arrangement that will perform well, for some time to come. Build in flexibility for future changes, if you are able practically to do so. Modern wireless communications will definitely ease the equipment arrangement and placement challenge.

Some movers are experienced in computer relocation. Seek out the professionals in the business and pay for their expertise.

Back up files, of course, on a server that won't be impacted.

♦ ♦ ♦

D. Floor Layout Drawings

Is there a floor layout of the existing facility? Of the new facility? An accurate inventory of equipment? Do not assume they are correct, at your peril.

Building layouts tend to be much easier in this age of computer aided design. But a computer layout was initially generated by a person with a tape measure. It may or may not have been kept up to date. My experience tells me that no layout drawing is absolutely correct. There may be only one error but if that is important to your plan, it is serious.

♦ ♦ ♦

E. Telephone Systems

Is there a new phone number or is the present one to be relocated? In either case you are dependent on the phone company and that is scary. Keep the phone company under close, personal oversight and on a short leash.

The best bet is to have the new phones installed and operating in the destination in advance. That is easy if the phone number is new. You will be told it is impossible if the number is the same but challenge the phone company as high up as you can get to make it happen, perhaps as a separate set of extensions. Make them innovate.

If the Phone Company insists on a change the day of the move, called a cutover, check their plans and backups closely. Get assurances that their people will be authorized overtime to stay with the project to correct any problems.
You may buy the switchboard through a different company that the company you buy service from, setting up a scenario where each can point fingers at the other when problems arise. There is no magic advice for that possibility, just be aware it can happen, allow enough time, and try to specify responsibility.

♦ ♦ ♦

F. Moving Insurance

You will face the question of insurance for the equipment that you relocate while it is the mover's responsibility. There is no one constant answer, yes you should insure or no, you needn't. Nor will you have a firm idea of the dollar limits of the policy. The cost will be higher than you think is necessary, and you will consider the possibility of a problem to be slight.

But you must balance the cost and likelihood of loss against the size of the risk and the damage to your business if a moving van were to be in an accident, or a computer CPU dropped.

♦ ♦ ♦

G. Security

Moves are not business as usual, and otherwise rigid security rules may be relaxed unintentionally. Be sure to protect the confidential aspects and intellectual property of the business during a move, as well as the physical assets.

♦ ♦ ♦

H. Move-in Path

I have been burned by this detail, so I'll prepare you. Scope out the route material will take, out of the source and into the destination. Changes of elevation can be challenging. Consider height of openings as well as width, floor load capacity, all impedances to a rolling wheel. If you will use a truck with a lift gate, be advised that all lift gates are not created equal, and ones that rest flat and close to the surface are distinctly easier and safer than others.

◆ ◆ ◆

I. In and Out

Put-away is just as important and time consuming as pack-it-up. If the same people who packed will also unpack, put-away will be smoother than if there are different sets of people.

In either case, record what is packed and where, how it will be moved and when, and where it will be placed at the destination. Mark the container with the destination coordinates.

Understand exactly what the moving people will do, and the point at which employees just take over put-away tasks. Have an adequate crew to handle the material, and dispatch it directly to the final location. In case an intermediate location must be used, keep good records.

Should you clean out the files before a move? Good idea; there will be less to move. But don't take the action just for the move; do it in accordance with sound business practice and
according to your company policy and legal retention requirements.

◆ ◆ ◆

Chapter 7   Relocate for cost reasons

or to access qualified employees or support.

A. There *will* be costs and there *may* be benefits

It is certainly possible for a business to cost justify another facility, instead of or in addition to, because of location-sensitive operating costs, community incentives and tax combination, regulatory climate. Access to qualified employees or specialized vendors and support is another reason for a company to urgently seek another locale even in a poor economy, in order to maintain product volume or quality.

For cost justification, the characteristics of your company will determine what costs can be lower in another community, and if a payback is possible after relocation cost.

Placing multiple entities in one location can allow reductions in administrative and shared costs. These consolidation reductions are called economies of scale, or synergy, or paradigm shift or whatever today's popular term is. It is certainly possible to reduce costs this way, but perhaps they can be reduced by a determined and skillful effort without a move. I have also seen operations which most involved believed had outgrown their optimum size. The following specific guidelines will help point out just where organizational benefits can outweigh costs.

In a relocation or expansion, there WILL be short term costs. There MAY be long term benefits.

A company will need to identify, quantify and compare one-time and operating costs and benefits at the current and alternative new locations, then calculate the net financial payback of each alternative. Be sure to consider:

1. Direct and indirect headcount at all levels of the organization: cost of pay; cost to hire and train at the destination, cost of an attrition plan or termination at the source.

2. Buy or build or lease space in the facility for: Equipment, operation, inventory, headcount related, maintenance, other support and administration.

3. Equipment added for operation, purchase and depreciation, tooling

4. Utilities and energy, including waste treatment, waste disposal and emissions

5. Transportation in and out; and this variable is increasingly important in the time of rising fuel costs.

6. Regulatory cost of being a resident of a particular state and community, and those costs vary dramatically.

7. Startup costs: to disconnect, move, reconnect, train, absorb learning curve losses; for travel, for process qualification and validation. Technology transfer costs usually increase as complexity of the operation increases. Cost of the move itself increase as machinery size, weight, plumbing and foundations increase.

8. Cost of closedown at the source, and any property actions.

9. Possible interruption to channels of supply

10. Costs of actions to avoid business interruption, such as inventory buildup, or parallel operation of facilities.

11. Taxes and the offset of relocation incentives which can possibly be negotiated with the state or community. More than ever, states may offer incentives to retain jobs.

◆ ◆ ◆

B. Where, exactly?

For access to people, vendors and support, the characteristics of your company will determine what communities could offer resources more attractively than the present base. There is a vast infrastructure who would attract your organization to their community, and all want to profit from your presence. I'll have another book on the subject soon, and meantime will continue to assist to find the best community for an organization's objective and subjective requests.

One guiding principle in this phase is to keep confidentiality. Do not divulge the corporate identity or purpose until you are ready to take a public stance. An organization has the most cost and bargaining leverage when it is unidentified. In this regard, an objective consultant with no stake in the community can easily maintain confidentiality.

◆ ◆ ◆

C. People

One of the most significant considerations in facility location is the availability of qualified employees. The unemployment rate in a community is important and easily quantified. Whether or not there are potential employees suited for your business is another question, much more difficult to evaluate in advance.

First, what kind of skills requirements does your company have? And are you able to meet that requirement where you are?

Does the educational system provide people trained to the level you need, generally? In a community you consider? Will you pay to relocate skills from another location? Can you train employees in the skills? Is training one of the incentives that a community will provide? (Training subsidies are quite common.)

♦ ♦ ♦

D. Support

Tough questions should be asked about the availability of specialized vendors and support that you will require in the community you choose. There are many technology centers in the US, areas such as Silicon Valley in California; a similar community near Boston; Research Triangle in North Carolina; Austin. Large cities sponsor attempts to create such centers, in one or another technology, in their vicinity. These centers can provide services just across the street that are vital to the success of a company, so be sure that you understand the importance of support that you depend on. In this day of overnight package service, perhaps local support is not as important as before but check it out.

♦ ♦ ♦

E. Quality of life

Don't overlook quality of life, and not just for the corporate executives who will live in a location. QOL will help you attract the kind of people you want. But, QOL is in the eye of the beholder; one size does not fit all.

♦ ♦ ♦

Chapter 8   Risk management

Most aspects of business in the 21st century must consider risk management, and the practice of facility planning can require the same treatment, it seems. The primary message is that even actions that appear to be innocuous should be at least briefly reviewed for the possibility that they may cause serious damage to the corporation; today or in the future.

Be extremely aware of how very high costs can occur, inside the facility or later as a result of facility output. (Think missed schedules, property lawsuits.) Double down on safeguards to prevent loss now or later.

◆ ◆ ◆

The primary purpose of this chapter is to raise the level of awareness, not to present a list of proscribed practices. Nevertheless, a brief review of historical events, from the media and from personal experience, highlights a few good examples of bad examples.

An important factor to remember is that standards change. An action taken at one time may well have been perfectly legal and not out of limits as far as community concerns were stated. Later on, laws and values shift.

A. Facility planning, especially site selection.

The location of some future natural disasters are hard to predict; tornados for one. Others tend to be predictable, and don't think it can't happen to you. Avoid construction in earthquake zones, on coasts subject to tidal waves, hurricane-prone areas, flood plains.

If you build in what is now rural country side, keep the trees cut back so a forest fire won't get to the facility; buy surrounding property so than neighborhoods won't sprout across the street from your hazardous process.

Avoid property that can become scenic or recreational; the newcomers will want you to vacate.

Multi-story buildings that collapse in Bangladesh didn't fail because of a plant layout, and the real story is human tragedy and not facility planning. Just don't let your shortsightedness lead you into such a situation.

◆ ◆ ◆

B. Environmental issues

Asbestos and lead in buildings will lead to cleanup or disposition cost sooner or later. If they are in property that you own or administer the cost will likely be sooner. Be sure that you do not acquire property with asbestos or lead; have EPA Phase I, II, or III inspections to confirm the content of property before acquisition.

Property where past activities left environmental hazards in the residue falls in the same category. Technology is available now to minimize the issues and cost, but deal only with certified experts.

So-called "brownfield" sites have been contaminated previously, and communities or owners seek to have them cleaned and put back in use. The property may be located or priced so that it could be useful for your organization, but again, deal only with certified experts.

◆ ◆ ◆

C. Dates

1. Dates in legal documents must be considered a red alert priority; respect them. Know when an activity is required and act sooner. Risk rises should you miss a lease date for instance, or fail to fulfill a contractual obligation.

In the mountain town where I spend summers, a ski resort inexplicably missed a renewal date for thousands of acres of ski slopes, and if they are able to renew at all, their rent will likely jump, add at least another zero at the end.

2. Dates in project management may be set by executive decision. My guidance is to set dates after considering what is to be done, and the workload of the resources left to do it.

◆ ◆ ◆

Chapter 9   Glossary of layout terms

These terms apply across all aspects of layout, floor plan and facility design.

8 Conditions for Flow Production, Hiroyuki Hirano
Condition 1: To lay out the facilities in the sequence of the process.

Condition 2: To make facilities small and exclusive use.

Condition 3: U-shape line / parallel line.

Condition 4: Working by standing.

Condition 5: Multi-process operation, multi-skill operator.

Condition 6: To bring up the degree of processing one by one.

Condition 7. Synchronization.

Condition 8: To make the flow clean.

18 Principles of Flow Production, Frank G. Wollard
1. a) Mass production demands mass consumption.
     b) Flow production requires continuity of demand.

2. The products of the system must be specialized.

3. The products of the system must be standardized.

4. The products of the system must be simplified in general and in detail.

5. All material supplies must conform to specification.

6. All supplies must be delivered to strict timetable.

7. The machines must be continually fed with sound material.

8. Processing must be progressive and continuous.

9. A time cycle must be set and maintained.

10. Operations must be based on motion study and time study.

11. Accuracy of work must be strictly maintained.

12. Long-term planning, based on precise knowledge, is essential.

15. Every activity must be studied for the economic application of power.

16. Information on costs must be promptly available.

17. Machines should be designed to suit the tasks they perform.

18. The system of production must benefit everyone – consumers, workers, and owners.

Aisle   An open passageway through a facility, designed to expedite movement of people and materials,

Block layout   The first layout type to be created, which considers groups or functions or departments in a building but not individual workstations. The "block layout" will be an arrangement of all the groupings in a facility, in order a) to show that all will fit in the area available; and b) to plan for the most effective flow and positioning of blocks within a building relative to each other and to building features. See Block layout chapter 47.

CAD Computer Aided Design, electronic creation of drawings, including layout and equipment. Modern versions are 3D, and allow creation of layers, for integrated views of under-floor and overhead, for instance plumbing and HVAC and wiring. See chapter 48

Cellular manufacturing   An approach in which manufacturing work centers (cells) have the total capabilities needed to produce an item or group of similar items. Cellular contrasts to setting up "modular" work centers on the basis of similar equipment or capabilities, in which case products must move among multiple work centers before they are completed.

Certification   Equipment and process may need to be certified or validated before production internally, or in some regulated industry. Build the step into timetables.

Checkers game   A succession of moves to implement a layout, only possible if there is an empty position to begin with. First relocate to an empty location, then into the position vacated by the first move, and so on.

Commissioning is the final step for major purchase orders of equipment, before a vendor turns over equipment. The buyer will need to provide a finished workspace, power, lights, product, etc. so be sure to include the step in the critical path.

Coordinates   Position of a location on a layout. Label each building column, by letters one way and numbers the other, to create the coordinates grid on the plant layout.

Consolidation of facilities   Whether or not an economy is shrinking, benefits can often be gained by consolidating or integrating facilities. There may be synergies possible from combination of equipment, floor space, capacity, technical acumen; from longer runs; from lower levels of facility-related management and overhead; from integrated scheduling, purchasing; from distribution patterns and methods. See chapter 62.

Destination   The position to which an operation will be moved. Typically it is the destination which is the subject of a layout. See chapter 54.

Detailed layout   The final layout, to reach the optimum arrangement of equipment within a work area. Each piece of equipment, each work station, is placed into a precise location for effective and productive output. A detailed layout will show utility connections, support equipment and inventory locations. The detailed layout requires considerable development because it precedes integrated placement of equipment and interconnection to utilities, which is why it is not started until the Block Layout is finalized. See "Block, and Detailed Layout" chapter 47.

Dimensions   Specific measurements of buildings, equipment and furnishings. Accurate dimensions are absolutely key to creation of effective layouts. Existing layouts are notoriously prone to dimensional error; confirm rather than just accept dimensions.

Dock   An entryway through which material is transferred between a vehicle and a facility, either arriving or departing the facility.

Drawing   A document which displays the relationship and dimensions of a facility, or equipment.

Flow, work flow   The movement of materials and people within an operating system Direct, straightforward flow is a prime goal of effective layout. See chapter 52.

Flow chart   "Flow chart" may be the process of graphically displaying the steps of an operation, or it may refer to the diagram itself. For many including me the first step to understanding an operation is to flow chart it.

There are only five things that can occur during a step in a process; an operation, a move, a delay, an inspection, a storage. Note that four of these possibilities do not add value. Work of any type can be flow charted; products, paperwork, electronic documents.

Geometry   The sizes and shapes which affect a layout, of the building and of the components to be placed in the building or facility.

Lean manufacturing or lean production; the philosophy of continually reducing waste in all areas and in all forms; an English phrase coined to summarize the Toyota Production System. See chapter 84.

Materials handling   Transportation of the components involved in the operation, often a major limitation on the available options for equipment arrangement. The term may include trays, bins, carts, conveyors, pallets, racks, totes, lift trucks, over-the-road trucks; or larger equipment such as cranes, among others.

Manual layout   Creation of a layout by hand, without use of computer drawings.

Master plan   A facility master plan layout is the arrangement of all of the components required for a business to perform its charter. It is the broad view of design, layout, and the arrangement of functions and departments, rather than the detail of people, materials and machines.

Master planning may be tailored to a property, to a building, or to an entire campus, depending on an organization's objectives. If the facility is only one building, the Master Plan will essentially be the same as a Block layout. See "Master Plan" chapters 56 and 73.

Move The physical relocation itself, from one location to another. A natural result of layout. See chapter 55.

Move-in, move-out path   The route that will be taken as an operation is relocated from one point to another. Width, height, floor load, elevation changes are key.

Office move   A move of office or administration functions follows the general layout rules, with some unique elements. See chapter 58.

Origin, source   The position from which an operation will be moved.

Outgoing waste   Solid, liquid, gas which may or not require environmental treatment. Sanitary, process, or waste water drains. Exhaust fans, scrubbers. Solid waste, scrap product.

Ownership   1) who has the rights to the floor space. 2) all of the stake holders, those affected by a layout. See chapter 51.

Paper-doll   A scale drawing template of an object, equipment, rack, furnishing or other component of a layout. Templates are cut out and positioned on a layout drawing to create an effective and graphic arrangement of components which can be easily modified, to recognize "what-if" scenarios. Drawings are then made of the favored template layout. See chapter 48.

Permanent facilities   Facilities or functions not easily relocated, such as docks, rest rooms, steam generators, water or waste treatment, chemical processes, storage tanks or silos, drain fields. Place these where there is minimum likelihood they will need to be relocated in the future. Never place them in the path of future expansion.

Process   A sequence of events, flow or product, or group of operations.

Revision   A change, as in a new version of a previous document such as a layout.

Security   Moves are not business as usual, and otherwise rigid security rules may be relaxed unintentionally. Be sure to protect the confidential aspects and intellectual property of the business during a move, as well as the physical assets.

Simulation programs, computer based, can help to evaluate layout options. Formal systems are on the market which will "simulate" actual manufacturing results by performing many iterations in an electronic model rapidly. The user plugs in values to selected operating variables, a program performs large numbers of iterations, and results predict performance of production lines. It is practical to change a variable's value to learn the impact of the change.

Spaghetti flow   An irregular and inefficient flow of materials, which continually doubles back on or across itself. In Asia, amend this term to Noodle Flow.

Straight line flow   Direct movement of materials and product without significant variation in the line, normally the most efficient option. Can be U shaped or L shaped, for instance to follow building walls, or start and stop near the same location.

Technology transfer   Relocation of the factors of an operation which, because it is technical in nature, may be more complex. Documentation and trained operators are key. See chapter 53.

Template   A scale drawing of an object, equipment, rack, furnishing or other component of a layout. It will be positioned on a layout drawing to create an effective arrangement of components.

U-shaped flow   Direct movement of materials and product through a facility, with changes of direction so that material leaves near where it entered.

Utilities   Supplies such as electricity, water, gas, high pressure air, steam, vacuum.

Validation   Equipment and process may need to be certified or validated before production internally, or in some regulated industry. Build the step into timetables.

Visible inventory, of which the JIT term Kanban is an example. All the inventory is on the production floor in sight so that there should be no surprises, no unexpected surplus or shortage. This almost always contributes to superior flow compared to moving material in and out of a remote inventory spot, but it needs the space near to production.

Work station   A location for performance of a task or operation. May be a machine, desk, service or assembly point, computer, office, sales counter, maintenance bench, service center, lab bench, conveyor belt, control panel.

Workplace layout   The arrangement of the tools, equipment, and materials that are present at a work station, and their relationship to the person or persons who operate them and produce a product. See chapter 57.

Chapter 10   If you only read one layout chapter

These topics are covered individually in other chapters of the Layout section. They are summarized here in one place to suggest that these are the imperative actions. The imperatives will contribute extensively to your specific objectives, but remember not all layout projects are the same.

A. Plant layouts tend to be infrequent, designed to catch up to changes in equipment, products, volumes, and flow. Get it right, the next one may not occur for a while.

◆ ◆ ◆

B. For an effective new layout, first pull out all of the waste movement, unnecessary material handling. Material flow, or routing through the process, will then dictate the sequence of equipment as it does with any successful layout.

◆ ◆ ◆

C. Create plans that satisfy not only current but also future space demands.

◆ ◆ ◆

D. Place work stations and inventory to amplify their interactions.

◆ ◆ ◆

E. Arrange for short and direct material flow paths.

◆ ◆ ◆

F. Simplify organization of material from receiving through shipping. Don't forget safety, and access for equipment operation and upkeep.

◆ ◆ ◆

G. The keyword is utilization; of space of course but also of equipment where it can serve multiple products; of storage through low inventories; of work through intelligent process flow and proximity of functions.

◆ ◆ ◆

H. A lean layout will tend to have a straight-line flow, little in-process inventory, more special purpose machines and ready access to all ancillary materials for quick changeover and flexible operations. Some people ask about a "lean" layout, when they don't have a "lean" process. My advice is to achieve a lean operation first, and then lay it out. You won't be successful if you don't have a lean operation, but try to attain it just through layout.

♦ ♦ ♦

I. When you include all the stake holders in the development process, the new layout will very likely be more well suited to real conditions, you'll put it into effect more smoothly, and stake holders will work to make it successful.

♦ ♦ ♦

J. Create layouts to accommodate new technology, additional products or volume.

♦ ♦ ♦

K. Apply productivity principles to create an effective arrangement and work flow; minimize space constraints.

♦ ♦ ♦

L. It is very common to execute a relocation with a "checkers" game, a series of sequential moves. But there has to be an empty space on your checkerboard to start with. First move into the empty space, then move something else into the just-vacated space, and so on. Phased projects are common, as are sequential moves.

♦ ♦ ♦

M. Corporate strategy may suggest a move from point A to point B. When this happens, take advantage of the move to create a point B layout with advantageous operating practices, tailoring your process to the facility dimensions.

♦ ♦ ♦

N. Office layouts are a special case because they usually are quite visible, and affect both clients and executives. Timing to cut business interference is usually critical and employees can really contribute with planning and execution.

O. Layouts for a particular function, perhaps maintenance or storage or office, require less time but utilize the same basic layout principles as a larger project.

◆ ◆ ◆

P. If there is a need for building modifications to accommodate a layout, that may control the timeline. Permits, approvals, and the modifications themselves tend to take more time than anticipated. Regulatory requirement for building and process will almost always extend timelines.

◆ ◆ ◆

Chapter 11   Step one, to create a layout

A non-negotiable checklist, for the one who will prepare the layout

Prepare the following, more or less in the order indicated, or later you will waste time or create an incorrect layout. Is this strong enough advice? Do it or else you will wish you had.

Make a record of all judgments rendered during this phase, as part of the "assumptions". When a decision is made, record the person who takes responsibility for the assumption. (There will be assumptions which prove to be incorrect, and when this happens formally change the assumption, and move on. Layouts by nature are a process, that changes over time.) Record dates and revision levels of official documents.

A. First, understand management's objectives and priorities completely.

This understanding will include what, where, and when. It may also involve "what next" if subsequent moves will occur.

◆ ◆ ◆

B. Obtain a drawing of the existing and destination buildings,
the "as built" and any other buildings that will be a part of the final plan.

1. Be sure that drawings are correct, that actual measurements match those on the drawing. Do not accept that drawing are correct without confirmation, at your peril. "As builts" are notoriously incorrect.

2. Is the drawing made by hand or by computer? What scale is it? Best is a CAD plot, where scale may be modified; if the drawing is manual, can it be converted to CAD? Small scale, 1/16 inch equals 1 foot, or the metric equivalent, is acceptable for "block" layouts, but for "detail" layout, a larger scale is necessary in order to illustrate the dimensions for equipment placement, and utilities installation, etc.

3. Confirm not only building dimensions, but also locations of permanent, fixed objects; such as docks, doors, stairways, elevators, drains, plating, water and waste treatment, HVAC, rest rooms, load bearing walls. Record restrictions such as floor loads, door and ceiling heights.

◆ ◆ ◆

C. Resolve any future expansion plan for a facility.

If the facility is to be expanded, look at the options and decide whether to leave space throughout the layout for later use, or to set an expansion direction and leave it available until it is later used.

◆ ◆ ◆

D. Required input for layout planning

A practical solution for the layout planner is to require each department to list all of the parameters that apply to them. Place this responsibility on the ones who will occupy the space. This does not mean that the plan is cast in concrete as changes can always be expected. But it is easier to change a paper layout, than to change bricks and concrete.

Make a list of the parameters, monitor what is turned in and what not, and attach a formal list of requested and available assumptions to each layout. Include such as:

1. Each department lists their own equipment, work stations, material handling aides, stores, supplies, and tools that the department will place in the new layout, both at first and in the future.

2. Each department lists its flow chart, what steps are required, and where; by product and by model.

Even a correct router may not indicate the inventory locations between steps, so add in to the flow path all storage locations for raw material, in-process and finished goods. Consider batch sizes, in-process storage, whether just in time or just in case; quantities to be kept; incoming and outgoing staging or kan-bans. Assure that all quality checks are marked on the flow plan. Where is the product kept during the quality check, and in case it is held up or quarantined or returned to vendor?

3. Each department lists any other departments, functions, support activity that should be located nearby because of product flow or material movement, shared supervision, support. List any that should be far off, because of noise, radiation, vibration, etc.

◆ ◆ ◆

E. Utilities and waste products

Determine for the process all utility feeds required from outside the facility, and sizes of supply line. Identify waste material products and quantities.

◆ ◆ ◆

F. Obtain layouts of emergency routes and exits,

Verify aisle widths defined by policy or required by law, measure what the material handling equipment actually requires, straight line and turning and right-angle access. Conform to these restrictions.

◆ ◆ ◆

These actions won't assure a good layout, but they will get you off to a comprehensive, professional, objective, start.

◆ ◆ ◆

Chapter 12   What is the degree of difficulty?

The purpose of this chapter is to point out factors that experience has proven to affect the scope and Degree Of Difficulty of a layout project. Where "DOD" is noted on a question, if the answer to a question is yes, expect a degree of difficulty. Consider all answers however, for their impact on your project.

Also, for every layout there will presumably be a destination and a subsequent relocation. Many of these questions involve destination or relocation.

A. Scope (The larger the answer, the higher the DOD)

Number of people in total
Private offices
Cubicles
Work areas, square feet
Reception, lobby, building admin
Amenities, square feet
How many moves in sequence are planned?
Distance between source and destination for a move?

♦ ♦ ♦

B. Site search if another building is to be used

Has the company made known its intention to relocate, to employees; to the public? If no, do it and the sooner the better.

Desire to lease or own (DOD) the destination?

General location of search, distance from origin?

General condition of real estate market in the area today?
Is it expected that property acquired will require extensive modification? (DOD)
Who will design any modifications, who will manage the construction?
Is it expected that property acquired will require zoning change or construction permits? (DOD)

♦ ♦ ♦

C. Telecommunications

Computer mainframe involved? (DOD)
Desire new hardware or software at the time of the move? (This is a Double DOD; just don't do it. Put the new gear in before or after, not during.)
Destination to be wired for computer?
Incoming lines on telephone switchboard
Intend to move the switchboard or procure a new one?
Other incoming connections; cable,

◆ ◆ ◆

D. Timing
What is the target date for a move?
Is it fixed, as a lease expiring? (The sooner, the greater DOD)
Must the organization remain open for business during the transition? (DOD)
Is the project size such that the transition will be performed over a time period?
Can / should the move itself be phased? Well considered phases can often ease the DOD.

◆ ◆ ◆

E. Logistics
Will current employees move with the business, minimizing technology transfer issues? (If not the degree of difficulty rises.)
Does the company expect to have employees assist with packing and unpacking? (DOD drops if the same employees both pack and unpack the same cartons.)
Is the company prepared to take possession of the destination early for modification? (Earlier is better to lower DOD)
Are there any furniture, furnishings, equipment large, or heavy, or technical, that might require riggers and not just a moving company?
Any off-premises furniture, furnishings, storage to be assimilated at the destination?
Loading dock available for movers?
Freight or passenger elevators on the move path? Note their weight limits, door and floor sizes.
Any unusual cleanup required of the vacated premises, especially if hazardous waste (DOD)?

Is CAD - CAM   now used for layout purposes? Is it available? If not, the technical aspects of the layout will take longer and be less reliable.

F. Complexity of technology to be relocated

Is documentation in place so that operators at the destination can perform the work? Will some operators not relocate? (DOD)

◆ ◆ ◆

G. Status of destination facility.

Availability before target move day; longer is better.

◆ ◆ ◆

Chapter 13   Block layout, and detailed layout

This chapter explains the strategy for block and detailed layouts, and their differences and uses. *Chapter 52 presents specific hands-on actions to implement both types of layouts.*

A block layout is the first layout type, which creates the "big picture" arrangement of departments, functions, and product flow; the detailed layout which follows itemizes exact arrangement of equipment and furnishings within a work area.

The block layout determines the overall dimensions of an group of activities or department and draws them as one piece, a "block" of floor space. The detailed layout sets each piece of equipment, each work station, into a precise location for effective and productive output. It will show utility connections, support equipment and inventory locations.

A. Block Layout Concept

A block layout is very useful to evaluate, and to differentiate, general arrangement options within a building. It will allow flow planning between groups or functions. It will also make sure that all pieces of the operation will fit into the chosen area in the first place.

Block layout provides a visual aid to compare how different arrangements would provide for production efficiencies, flow, space utilization, growth, access. A block layout before final selection can also point out necessary leasehold improvements and modification, for instance electrical distribution or drains, walls or doors.

♦ ♦ ♦

B. A Plan for a Block Layout Phase

1. Have managers quantify their specific needs in the destination area. Some factors address space requirements, some positioning.

a. Total space required; will include materials in, processes and equipment, in-process inventory, packing process and packaging material, finished goods, department admin.

b. Relationships of a department to another department.

c. Future expansion plans for a facility. If the facility is to be expanded, decide whether to leave space throughout the layout for later use, or to set an expansion direction and leave it available until it is later used.

d. Permanent, fixed building features. Position them so that they do not interfere with flow today, nor lie in the path of future expansion plans.

e. Distribution of utilities; power, water hot or cold, drains or chemical drains, HP air. If possible group heavy users near the utility source to avoid extra use of buss bar, or piping, or drains.

f. Volume of materials received; if heavy volume, provide good access to receiving.

g. Volume of materials shipped; if heavy volume, provide good access to shipping,

h. Different receiving and shipping doors for different products.

i. Do departments share an inventory location, or do they store dedicated materials?

j. Equipment on the computer server, and controls.

k. Waste generated, exhaust requirements. Climate control circumstances.

l. Any shortage or surplus space today? Expected future changes, in technology, volume, product?

m. Idle equipment that should be kept for backup and capacity?

n. Ceiling heights required. Floor loading. Special lighting. Electronic frequency generation.

2. Prepare a layout of the destination area, a CAD drawing if it is available, otherwise create one.

3. Determine the floor area for each department or function which will occupy the facility. Create templates of the floor area to the same scale as the destination footprint.

4. Position blocks representing department or functional areas on the footprint, to develop a facility block layout. Consider general flow, access to aisles and docks, relationships of functions that interact, proximity to utilities and drains, etc.

5. When you have created a good option, copy it and create other options. Layout options are ideally suited for visual analysis that all can understand. As a practical matter, find a place where you can leave the layout and options on display, in a project room. In order to explore new options easily, spread the footprint drawing on a horizontal surface, and provide templates for the stakeholders to arrange,

Bring in stakeholders to evaluate the operating effectiveness of each option, gather around the table, place templates on the footprint and let the group contribute. Judge the options considering all the objective and subjective information, suggest other options and provide feedback. Repeat until the most favorable option is selected. Obtain signatures. There may still be changes, but record that all concerned have approved for the record.

♦ ♦ ♦

C. Detailed Layout Concept

A detailed layout will eventually be necessary, to define exactly where each machine and rack and desk will be placed and connected to services and utilities. At that time you may well find that the final revision is not quite identical to the block layout, so modify and adjust as necessary.

The detailed layout will involve accurate measurements of equipment and furnishings, as all contents of the operation must be drawn in their final position, The detailed layout will guide final installation of components, relative to each other, and to existing building walls and doors and aisles and columns and pipes and drains. Measure carefully for both equipment and facility.

♦ ♦ ♦

D. A Plan for a Detailed Layout Phase

Prepare the facility layout, using a CAD drawing if it is available, otherwise create one. Draw it exactly as it exists. Use a scale of 1/4" or 1/8" equals one foot (or equivalent metric), to provide enough detail for pipe and wire connections for instance.

Create a template for each piece of equipment or furnishing, inventory location, discrete object that requires floor space. Turn equipment the correct way for operator position and product flow. Be sure that access is not constrained. Try various arrangements to find the most suitable considering the layout objectives.

When you have a good option, copy it and create other options. Then bring in the stakeholders to evaluate the operating effectiveness of each option, judge the options considering all the objective and subjective information, and provide feedback. Repeat until the most favorable is selected. Obtain signatures. There may still be changes, but record that all concerned have approved for the record.

Once the final arrangement is chosen, add detail to show information to install the layout, primarily utilities feeds, drains, etc. Consult closely with the maintenance people who will install, and provide the detail they need.

◆ ◆ ◆

E. Three Dimensions, and Outside the Walls

Layout is typically two dimensional, but do not forget height.

Within the facility, assure that each equipment and workplace has enough room for its vertical dimension, and for access into it for operation or maintenance in all three dimensions.

1. Many buildings can effectively utilize multiple floors. Vertical flow can be very effective.

2. Supplies can be located outside to good effect.

3. Do not forget that outside storage can block expansion of the facility in that area.

◆ ◆ ◆

Chapter 14   What format, CAD or paper-dolls?

Templates, if you don't want to play with paper-dolls.

Or maybe both. The answer depends somewhat on your own present practice.

A. CAD, computer aided design, has been a major advance for plant layout.

1. There are several commercially available systems, AutoCad and Siemens produce the most popular programs.

CAD programs offer many advantages; the ability to change a complex print quickly then print out the latest ranks very highly. The ability to change scale is very useful. Changes can be made easily. A facility really should have an integrated set of drawings, which CAD does easily. One layer of the integrated drawing is walls, another layer is aisles, another equipment, another emergency routes, another electrical, another plumbing, etc. Very neat, and now that we have it, indispensable for all of the components of plant architecture.

If your facility has CAD capability, you will find that layout and changes are easier from the drafting standpoint. Overall site planning is first performed, and it also is easier with CAD; see the Facility Planning section. For a plant, the first thing usually placed on a CAD file is the building itself; walls and columns and doors. The building drawing is the basis for any layout, and future change. Be sure that the layout is correct, that the building features are drawn correctly, to the right dimensions.

If equipment and furnishings are already drawn and on the CAD file, that saves a significant amount of time in the layout process. Again, confirm that drawings are correct. It may or may not be necessary to create a precise drawing of a machine or workstation or desk or rack, but a template of some accuracy will assure that a planned layout will actually translate to a workable arrangement when the equipment is placed into the destination.

2. Computerized mechanisms are available to optimize effective layout. There are commercial simulation programs at various levels of sophistication and cost; there are genetic layout algorithms for a more hands-on approach. Each performs multiple iterations to reach a preferred plan. In both cases the input requires that many factors which affect layout be recognized. Chapter 52, Tools, explains in greater detail.

◆ ◆ ◆

B. Paper-doll is a template of a piece of equipment, or a furnishing, or storage rack, or desk. Draw templates in CAD to the same scale as the building, print them, cut them out.

The old way to perform layouts was to prepare paper-doll templates of everything to go into an area with T-square and triangle, then fit them by hand onto the drawing of the area, to find the most effective arrangement. I still like to use paper-dolls, but CAD supplies the facility layout and the drawings that serve as equipment templates; I'll cut out templates and fit them into the CAD print. It is easy to try many optional arrangements quickly, and to change arrangements, to demonstrate what-if scenarios.

With paper dolls, just as in a CAD assisted layout, many factors which affect layout must be recognized. Computers can perform iterations quickly, and the persons involved can apply the many controlling factors from their experience.

One advantage of paper-dolls is that anyone can do it, and usually pretty well. Print a big CAD floor plan, cut out templates, and invite all concerned to arrange them. The best of both worlds.

I have seen groups of people solve layout dilemmas quickly. A major factor seems to that people can tailor a solution; for instance they can change a block that is 40' x 40'and doesn't fit into a corner, into a block 20' x 80' that does fit. They can figure out spatial relations and orientation quickly that would require re-entering data to a program.

♦ ♦ ♦

Chapter 15   Create layouts, explore options

Guidelines for the one who creates the layout

A. Understand the charter

First, understand management's objectives and priorities completely. That will include what, where, and when. It may also involve "what next" if subsequent moves will occur. Record the assumptions and requirements.

Define the requirements for use of the space, the contents, major access points, building limitations, regulations affecting the space including floor loads, rest rooms, fire codes and emergency routes.

Follow the concepts of the chapter 38, "Work Flow and Facility Layout" to achieve productive flow and layouts.

Plot several options as "block" layouts, discuss them with the stakeholders, and choose an efficient, safe, long lasting arrangement with good flow.

Finally, "detail" the block layout down to the level needed to install equipment, furnishings, utilities and connections.

After each layout is developed and before any subsequent actions are taken, get approvals in writing from all those concerned. This does not mean that the plan is cast in concrete as changes can always be expected. So a signed layout is valid only until a better one comes along; it's best to get it signed anyway.

◆ ◆ ◆

B. Basic concepts

A successful layout considers the variable factors that define your circumstances and objectives, then creates a productive flow, then fits that flow into the physical geometry of your equipment and facilities. A good flow pattern for materials and people should be a driving force for any layout. It may not be possible to quantify the benefits, but many productive practices follow from a careful layout; materials movement without retracing steps, visibility of inventory and of work, easy access of direct and support people, superior material handling, safety, housekeeping, emergency routes.

A prerequisite to a layout is to define material handling into an area, considering material dimensions and weight, overhead lift, trucks, conveyors, etc. Also determine how utilities will be provided, because while overhead supply is much easier it also can block access to equipment and interfere with sight lines and vision.

The classic method to gain room is to move into storage space, warehouses for instance. That often can be a practical option, especially if an objective is also to reduce inventory.

The type of inventory system in use is a major factor early in a manufacturing layout. Will material be supplied Just in Case, the traditional Materials Requirement Planning technique, or will the focus be on a lean process, or Just In Time delivery? Know what system you will use, in order to assign the correct amount of space to materials, in the appropriate places.

♦ ♦ ♦

C. Floor layout drawings

This section may be repeated elsewhere; it is important.

Is there a floor layout of the existing facility? Of the new facility? An accurate inventory of equipment? Do not assume they are correct, at your peril.

Building layouts tend to be much easier in this age of computer aided design. But a computer layout was initially generated by a person with a tape measure. It may or may not have been kept up to date. My experience tells me that no layout drawing is absolutely correct. There may be only one error but if that is important to your plan, it is serious.

♦ ♦ ♦

D. Create options, then choose what you like

It is far easier to erase lines on a piece of paper, than to relocate. Just as the old carpentry adage says, to "Measure twice and cut once", be sure to get it right first.

Layout options are ideally suited for visual analysis that all can understand. Many can stand around the table, contribute, and compare. As a practical matter, find a place where you can leave the layout and options on display, in a project room. In order to explore new options easily, spread the footprint drawing on a horizontal surface, and provide templates for the stakeholders to arrange,

The "block" layout stage occurs first. Create a good concept and flow first, agree on it and later convert it to a detailed layout.

Layouts tend to proceed in a circular process; as each phase adds knowledge. That sometimes means a previous step will have to be redone in light of new facts or insights. At each phase, note the assumptions that apply, for they may well change.

As a matter of good management practice, get all involved to initial the layouts. And of course keep copies of each layout iteration.

♦ ♦ ♦

E. Layout tools and techniques

Utilize the following tools and techniques to create effective layout options. These actions are not ranked, as their importance will not be the same in all situations. Their sequence may vary as well but consider the first few points early in the process.

1. An early layout step is to recognize fixed building features, such as under-floor plumbing, HVAC and vents, waste disposal, high and low ceilings and floor loads, restrooms, docks and access doors, employee entrances, major load bearing walls, utilities supply points, fixed outside storage containers, etc. Mark them on the layouts.

2. Position equipment which relates to fixed building features; and that relationship may be to interact with or to avoid.

3. Place fixed equipment, for instance those with foundations or piping or air handling or waste treatment, so that it can remain in place at the time of a future expansion or re-layout. (Even if the resulting flow is not totally efficient.)

4. Correct any building shortcomings at the time of a layout as the next rearrangement may not occur for a time.

5. Consider the locations of plant connections to energy and utilities; then reduce the internal distribution network if possible but product flow is usually a more important consideration.

6. Rearrange facilities and equipment to create shorter flow paths. Organize and cut through the "spaghetti" flow that adds distance and confusion. To the extent possible lay out operations as straight line or U shaped flow, even if flow has turns to accommodate

building geometry between receiving and shipping docks. Reduce product movement first and personnel secondarily.

Use routers and job tickets to identify the flow patterns for products. Give precedence to the most frequently used operations. Place inventory points between equipment in accordance with Just in Time or Just in Case inventory control used in the facility, sized accordingly.

Recognize preceding and following operations, as well as necessary support functions that interact.

7. Place work stations and inventory to amplify interactions of material and information flow with associated stations. Consider also negative features such as vibration, noise, heat and energy radiation, odor.

8. If there is space available to do so, assign unused floor sections throughout the process for future expansion. If a future action is identified, dedicate a space for it.

9. Make product flow and inventory through the process visible.

10. Reduce non-value-added activity such as handling by shortening distance to closely associated positions.

11. Plan comprehensively for movement of raw materials, in-process, and finished products throughout the operation including the handling system, aisle widths, and access to production equipment. Size storage areas according to the fundamental inventory control process employed in the facility.

12. Improve floor space utilization through appropriately sized aisles, and equipment positioning, within building constraints.

♦ ♦ ♦

F. Select a favorable layout and approve it

Create multiple layout options to demonstrate different ways to approach the overall objectives of the project, to show graphically how the necessary operations would fit into the facility and would interact with each other. If building additions are necessary, explore the possible positions on the site.

It is possible to assemble a presentation on a computer screen, but in my opinion a group of prints on paper is a superior technique; spread on the conference table or tape them to the walls and compare.

Review options with the stakeholders, and discuss. Be prepared for other options to be suggested, so have blank plans at hand for new thoughts.

Repeat the process until a decision is reached. This sequence can be used to review both block and detailed layout phases.

♦ ♦ ♦

G. Built-in material handling

Heavy duty material handling is often permanently mounted to the building. Gantry cranes, column-mounted traveling cranes, column-mounted jib cranes, permanent hoists, turn-tables, floor levelers, rails in a floor are examples. Conveyors may be fixed between equipment. Power doors, pass throughs, turntables may assist.

Often heavy handling equipment is related to heavy duty building construction, columns or girders or foundations.

The layout practitioner will have one of two situations; either to determine a layout so the building may be constructed, or to adapt a layout to an existing building configuration. Care is necessary either way. While layouts are often two dimensional, in the case of overhead equipment they are three dimensional. Also remember that not all floor space under an overhead span may be accessible for use.

If a layout is adapted to a building, the final flow choices may well be less efficient in order to conform to building characteristics.

♦ ♦ ♦

Chapter 16   Relationships of layout components

Near or far? Proximity may, or not, be important for departments, functions, groups.

Often it will be possible to locate an operation in one of several places. The final destination may be chosen because it is the most effective answer; because of product or people flow, or because of price, or because of future expansion, or because of proximity of shared input, or because of space utilization. Often a destination will be chosen because of relationships; proximity to a physical object, another department, a dock or elevator or drain; chemical or environmental treatment.

A. Simple Theory Of Relationships

A layout may have many components, ranging in size from a department to a machine or to an individual workplace. An effective layout will place components according to the relationships between them. If a process flows from one component to another, locate them close together. If a buyer meets with vendors, place purchasing near an outside door. If instruments are sensitive to vibration, don't place them near the punch presses.

♦ ♦ ♦

B. Components

Other chapters explain the difference between "Block" and "Detail" layouts. Components in a "Block" layout will be departments; components in a "Detail" layout will be machines and work stations. The theory of relationships is the same in each; determine the placement of a component depending on how it should interact with other components.

♦ ♦ ♦

C. Application of theory for both "block" and "detailed" layouts, in turn.

Relationships between components can sometimes be almost intuitive; in many cases it is quite easy to say that components should be together, or apart, or it doesn't matter, or "under no circumstances put them together".

An excellent mechanism for keeping track of the relationships on multiple components was developed by Richard Muther, now Richard Muther & Associates. It is called Simplified Systematic Layout Planning. Please see the company web site, for more information. http://www.hpcinc.com/rma/rma.asp,

Use a grid format to list components; triangular as Muther does, or across the top and down one side of a sheet of paper or spreadsheet. At the intersection of each pair of departments, decide how the departments relate to each other; the Simplified Systematic Layout Planning site suggests: absolutely necessary; especially important; important; okay; unimportant; undesirable. Judge the relationship of each component against each other one, and enter on the grid or spreadsheet.

Now assign a value to each relationship. Muther suggests a value of 16 for Absolutely necessary; 8 for Especially important; 4 for Important; 1 for Okay; zero for Unimportant; and a negative 80 value for Undesirable. To me the last rating is overkill, perhaps Undesirable should be equal to the highest favorable placement, negative 16. If there are two departments with a relationship of Undesirable, you are not going to place them close together anyway, are you. Choose the relationship values that seen right.

Rate all of the layouts options compared to the existing one, to determine how effective they are. First rate the existing one, later rate all options. In this manner you will create an objective way to compare layouts by how well they satisfy their functional relationships.

Rate layouts in this manner. Apply the numerical value to the spreadsheet or grid intersection, to quantify the relationship. Add up the values for all relationships, and compare the all options. The higher the number, the more effective the layout is from the standpoint of relationships.

♦ ♦ ♦

D. 3 Dimensions

If your layout is multi-story, there may be extremely good spatial relationship, where a product or component can flow downhill, from one department to another.

♦ ♦ ♦

E. Cautions

Spatial relationships are important. But there may be physical characteristics in your building that prevent a certain relationship, or increase the cost of it. For instance, the relationship diagram may suggest a department in a certain location, but that department is metal plating and there are no drains in the suggested location. Relationships may suggest shipping in a place where there are no docks or roads. Don't put a dynamic function in a corner with no room for growth, no matter what the relationship diagram says. Utilize a mezzanine, but not if the floor load limit is too low or the ceiling clearance inadequate.

Another caution is to consider what proximity of components really means. Is a relationship spatial or distance oriented, which would be important if a product moves from one place to another? Or for an objectionable feature; noise, or vibration, or odor, or energy radiation, it is possible to block the problem physically? What appears to be a difficulty may not be one at all.

◆ ◆ ◆

Chapter 17   Ownership in a layout

Ownership, in the layout context, has two meanings and you will be well advised to consider both of them for a smooth project with productive results. Ownership refers to 1) the rights to floor space, and 2) participation in the layout process itself by stakeholders.

A. Rights to the destination floor space

Management typically will have a reason for a relocation, usually centered around a need of the operation which will have a new layout.

In a checker game, moving from one space to another, remember that one space must be empty first. If that space is already empty, floor space ownership will be less significant. If all squares are full, the decisions will be more difficult; someone will own the intended destination. To the extent possible, make decisions by logic; let the data drive the decision.

A corollary, determining who pays for the layout and move, may rear its head in an interdepartmental disagreement. The premise "pusher pays" seems to work out well. Who is the champion of the idea? Put your money where your mouth is.

♦ ♦ ♦

B. Stakeholders

In a layout and subsequent change of location, quite often there are many stakeholders. The department itself (all involved, from bottom to top), those who service it, those who are fed by it, building and equipment maintenance, material handling may all have a voice.

Management has a stake of course. The people who prepare the layout are deeply involved, and will probably be the ones responsible for interaction with the other stakeholders. That will involve first getting a charter for action, finding out the details, learning from sources of objective information, discussions with sources of subjective information, informing all concerned of progress and expectations.

As in a democracy, not all stakeholders will necessarily be pleased with the result. Some facts will outweigh others in the formula to reach an intelligent decision; at best layout options may not be clearly defined. But keep stakeholders informed, what and when for sure, and to the extent possible why.

Chapter 18   Tools to apply, for successful layouts

This how-to chapter, specific guidance to apply the tools of the layout trade, is founded on the preceding chapters and incorporates them. The sections are arranged by the phases of the project where the tools will be the most useful. In some cases the tools may be repeated as they are appropriate in different sections of the book.

A. Before layout can even be considered

1. First, understand management's objectives and priorities completely. That will include what, where, and when. It may also involve "what next" if subsequent moves will occur. Assure that all are "singing from the same songbook". Record and communicate the assumptions and requirements.

2. Resolve any future expansion plan for a facility. If the facility is to be expanded, decide whether to leave space throughout the layout for later use, or to set an expansion direction and leave it available until it is later used.

3. Define the elements of the facility charter; parameters that apply, from topics such as:

a. What is the manufacturing model for the organization?
Batch, job shop, make to stock?

What delivery time is promised to the customer? This answer will dictate the extent of your inventory, especially in-process. A faster delivery promise may also require you to keep more raw materials on hand, but less finished goods.

b. What fundamental inventory control process is followed?
Will material be supplied <u>Just in Case</u>, the traditional Materials Requirement Planning technique, or will the focus be on a lean process, or <u>Just In Time</u> delivery? Some of each, for different materials? Know what system will be in use, in order to assign the correct amount of space to materials, in the appropriate places.

c. How will equipment be grouped? In a <u>Cell</u> arrangement, often used for JIT, equipment is often dedicated for a product or sequence and is grouped together accordingly. In the <u>Modular</u> arrangement, versatile equipment is grouped by function to process any product part; all the lathes together, all milling together, assembly in one place. In either case, define the batch size and material which will be stored at each workspace,

d. What expected capacity, widgets per time frame, is the planned layout to produce?

e. Obtain what defines incoming materials and outgoing products; a Bill of Materials

f. Obtain process documentation; router, flow chart.

Assure that all quality checks are marked on the flow plan. Where is the product kept during the quality check, and in case it is held up or quarantined or returned to vendor? Provide for this on the layout, and of course room for the quality check itself.

4. Make a special effort to eliminate waste throughout the plant. One of the major elements of Lean Manufacturing is to eliminate waste, so do it now to simplify operations and reduce handling for the overall layout project.

5. Once as much waste as possible has been eliminated, define *everything* that goes into the layout. This is vital, yet often not done well. All too often a layout is begun, long before it has defined the objectives and well before anyone has put together a list of the contents of an operation.

Require each department to list their own equipment, work stations, material handling aides, stores, supplies, and tools that the department will place in the new layout, both at first and in the future. Place this responsibility on the ones who will occupy the space. This does not mean that the plan is cast in concrete as changes can always be expected. But it is easier to change a paper layout, than to change bricks and concrete.

6. Document the product manufacturing process, and provide space for everything that is used.

Refer to the formal documents that define the components of the final product, flow patterns and assembly sequences. Apply Bills of Materials, routers, assembly diagrams, job tickets, inspection requirements. Not all products will be the same, so give precedence to the most frequently used operations.

Remember to provide space for non-product materials, for instance used packaging, scrap, return-to-vendor items.

7. As projects go forward, layouts tend to develop in a repeating process because each phase adds knowledge. That sometimes means a previous step will have to be redone in light of new facts or insights. At each phase, note the assumptions that apply, for they may well change.

8. <u>One extremely important concept to remember:</u>   Space planning is always dependent on product mix. Different models may not require the same materials, process, space or time frame.

There is no magic tool to deal with this fact. Just remember its importance and consider the affects as you plan today's layout, and tomorrow's.

◆ ◆ ◆

<u>B. Sequence of layout actions</u>

1. Obtain a computer file of the property. Obtain floor layouts of existing buildings. Access any existing computer files, from any source.

Confirm the accuracy of all layouts, property and floor. Do not assume they are correct, at your peril. Building layouts tend to be much easier in this age of computer aided design. But a computer layout was initially generated by a person with a tape measure. It may or may not have been kept up to date. My experience tells me that no layout drawing is absolutely correct. There may be only one error but if that is important to your plan, it is serious.

2. Plan to construct floor layouts within the building layout file, as one or more layers, so that floor layouts will interact with wiring, piping, columns, doors, etc.

In this manner, you can avoid interference between services, and arrange utilities to feed equipment precisely.

3. Define the requirements for use of the space, in two categories

Input-output diagrams can be very effective in this step. An I-O diagram is a graphical representation of all the factors that make up a process, to assure a comprehensive, accurate analysis. Make an I-O diagram of all inputs and all outputs, including scrap and emissions so that you can consider materials handling and flow for each. In succession, diagram the property, the building, the department. You will find that you can present concepts to others easily and effectively with input - output diagrams.

a. The property
Major access points, building limitations, regulations affecting the space including floor loads, rest rooms, fire codes and emergency routes. building functions and amenities such as food service, dorms, child care, medical, restrooms.

70

b. The contents,
Equipment, furnishings, offices, support, maintenance, quality, materials storage and staging, work stations, labs, shipping and receiving, security.

List everything you know or assume, not only to record what you have considered but also to make clear what has not been considered yet.

4. Develop several options as "block" layouts, discuss them with the stakeholders, and choose an efficient, safe, long lasting arrangement with good flow.

5. Using the favored "block" layout as the starting point develop several more specific options, layouts of equipment and workstations; discuss, and choose the best one. Continue to focus on product flow and relationships between components of the plan.

6. Finally, "detail" the chosen equipment and workstation layout down to the level needed to install individual machines, furnishings, utilities and connections.

Tradesmen will eventually install the equipment, tie it all together, prepare material handling, and connect it all together, using different CAD layers to detail the elements of the integrated layout.

The focus of the "detailed" layout shifts, to exact dimensions between equipment for clearance and interaction; workplace layout; to minimize distances in work patterns; operator position and ergonomics; containers and stands for product and parts; access for maintenance.

7. After each layout phase is developed and before any subsequent actions are taken, get approvals in writing from all those concerned even though later change is not unusual.

◆ ◆ ◆

C. Layout tools and concepts, for a previously used facility

1. Correct any building shortcomings at the time of a layout as the next rearrangement may not occur for a time. Widen, strengthen, resurface, re-roof, update.

2. Consider cost effective and rapid options such as expanding operations into storage space, warehouses for instance. This strategy can be practical, especially if an objective is

also to reduce inventory. Often warehouse space can easily be acquired and used off site, or as an add-on to the existing facility.

3. Recognize permanent, fixed building features, such as under-floor plumbing, HVAC and vents, waste disposal, high and low ceilings and floor loads, restrooms, docks and access doors, elevators, employee entrances, major load bearing walls, utilities supply points, fixed outside storage containers, etc.

Mark them on the layouts. Plan material flow with these features in mind, both for today's flow and to plan for a potential growth path in the future .

4. If the facility will be kept in operation during the installation of a new layout, consider a sequential, "checkerboard" move.

Relocate one operation at a time. Start with one empty space, move into it, then use the vacated space for the next move. A sequence will minimize down time during the transition.

◆ ◆ ◆

D. Ask managers to describe their requirements in the future layout

If only a small area is in question, concentrate on that. If larger areas of the facility are likely to be involved, show building services such as restrooms, point of utility distribution, break rooms, employee entrances, interior and exterior walls and doors, docks, property lines; location of each department, not the equipment or desk detail but dimensions, direction of product flow, main aisles, production and inventory sizes, potential expansion.

1. Require each department to list their own components that will occupy space; such as equipment, work stations, material handling aides, material stores, supplies, and tools that the department will place in the new layout, both at first and in the future. Be sure that all of the components are identified and listed. There is no way to recover from an omission.

a. Total space required is obviously critical; define materials in, processes and equipment, in-process inventory, packing process and packaging material, finished goods, department admin and control. Anything that uses floor space.

b. Any shortage or surplus space today? Assign room for growth based on expected future changes, in technology, volume, product characteristics.

c. Idle equipment that should be kept for backup and capacity? How is the equipment to be retained, in-place ready to operate or in a central mothballed storage?

2. Require each department to list the factors that determine where they should be placed, within the facility, identify any specific needs in the destination area.

a. Relationships of a department to another department, for maintenance, supervision, common technology, shared equipment or personnel, common materials; a reason for the departments to be near to each other after the move. Are there some that should be isolated, perhaps for reasons of noise, vibration, odors, energy radiation.

b. Use of utilities; power, water hot or cold, drains or chemical drains, HP air; group heavy users near the utility source to avoid extra use of buss bar, or piping, or drains.

c. Volume of materials received; if heavy volume, provide good access to receiving.

d. Volume of materials shipped; if heavy volume, provide good access to shipping,

e. Different receiving and shipping doors for different products; for pallet loads versus individual cartons? Might gain material handling efficiency but at the expense of central control.

f. Do departments share an inventory location, or do they store dedicated materials?

g. Equipment on the computer server, and controls.

h. Waste and exhaust requirements. Climate control circumstances, HVAC, heat or chemicals or fumes generated.

i. Ceiling heights required. Floor loading. Special lighting. Electronic frequency generation.

♦ ♦ ♦

E. Create a complete set of templates for the Block functions to be arranged.

This step is necessary whether the layout is to be constructed on a drawing board or a computer. This template set is for a "block" layout; departments, functions, areas; work, storage, inspection, movement.

(Another template set, machines, work places, conveyors, racks, bins, is suited for a "detailed" layout. and is only constructed, later in the layout process, when the Block layout is chosen. Many of the same steps are applied as for Block layout, but the emphasis is on machines and workspaces, not departments and functions.)

For both block and detail, print out the templates at the same scales as chosen for the building plans. In either set, create a template for <u>everything</u> that occupies floor space.

1. Process the information that was supplied by departments, in D. 1. above, of components to be in the layout.

Please note, that equipment and work stations tend to be identified readily. Other functions tend to be overlooked in planning stages. Confirm that the following are not overlooked:

a. Storage areas according to the fundamental inventory control process employed in the facility; just in time, or just in case.

b. Surge inventory, for temporary storage when one machine stops.

c. process and material flow staging between steps

d. quality checks, and associated staging, quarantine or return to vendor

e. Equipment that can be placed outside the facility walls; silos, tanks, hoppers

2. Determine the floor area of block templates
Although the block layout phase is early in a layout project, a substantial amount of work must be done to approximate the correct floor area of the templates.

This is especially true because the "block" layout is done before the "detailed" layout, but the floor area of the "block" depends on the contents of the "detail". A practical mechanism is to estimate the overall "block" size, from actual dimensions if the function already exists somewhere else, or to accumulate the list of components and determine each of their working dimensions. The benefit will occur however, as a more accurate "block" layout and an easier "detailed" layout process.

Among the useful actions to determine the size and shape of the areas required are

a. For a block layout, the accuracy level is not high, but consistent error on the small side will create an eventual problem, a cramped layout.

b. Determine the floor area required for each component listed. To the extent possible, refer to actual dimensions of equipment, work stations, conveyors, storage containers, interior aisles, operator and maintenance access, etc.

c. Apply the dimensions to the complete list of the components of the layout. Convert the dimensions into square feet.

d. The final total allowed area of the block may be:
    1. the addition of all square feet, all components to be included.

    2. the same as an area that is occupied now by the equipment, perhaps adjusted to recognize known shortages or extra space; or new or surplus equipment.

    3. supplied by a vendor, if new equipment is to be used.

    4. an arbitrary, assigned amount. (Very risky)

e. A template can be shaped by first determining the area, then by referring to the location of building walls and aisles. The final shape may be suggested by the portion of the building to be occupied, and whether that is straight or angled or fits into a corner.

◆ ◆ ◆

F. Develop a draft block layout for the facility

The block layout phase arranges all facility-wide functions, production and support departments, building services, employee amenities, receiving and shipping, internal traffic flow and storage, aisles.

1. Prepare a layout of the destination area, using a CAD drawing if it is available, otherwise create one. Draw it exactly as the facility exists. Use a scale of 1/8" equals one foot if possible (or equivalent metric), or 1/16" equals one foot. No smaller scale will typically suffice, even for a block layout.

2. Arrange the blocks for all departments and functions developed and sized, to reach a satisfactory end objective. Consider general flow, access to aisles and docks, relationship

to other functions that interact, proximity to utilities and drains, space utilization, future expansion, etc.

3. Sharpen the block layouts by techniques such as these:

a. Position fixed equipment so that it does not conflict with today's operation or tomorrow's expansion plan.

b. Solicit opinion from those to be involved, and modify, and develop options.

c. Expect that successive drafts will get progressively more accurate, and serve as guides for future layouts.

d. Determine how utilities will be provided internally. Overhead supply is much easier than under the floor but it also can block access to equipment by overhead material handling, as well as interfere with sight lines and vision. Locate incoming connections to plant-wide energy and utilities. Create a layout to reduce internal utility distribution network if possible to require less copper wiring, shorter pipes. Product flow is usually a more important consideration, but reduce distribution if possible.
.

e. Review the future expansion plan for a facility, and assure that the block layout follows the plan. Typically either leave space throughout the layout for later use, or set an expansion direction and leave it available.

f. Use a Flow Chart to understand the process and material flow. Absolutely resolve every step of the process. First, identify potential improvement and put it into effect with the layout. Involve a wide participation of people and disciplines during the analysis.

g. Arrange templates for departments and functions on the footprint plan, to create shorter flow paths between departments in the operating sequence. Organize and cut through the "spaghetti" flow that adds distance and confusion. To the extent possible lay out operations as straight line or U shaped flow, even if flow has turns to accommodate building geometry between receiving and shipping docks.

h. Place departments, functions and storage to amplify interactions of material and information flow. Recognize preceding and following departments, as well as necessary support functions that interact. Consider also negative features such as vibration, noise, heat and energy radiation, odor because they may suggest a longer distance separation.

i. If there is space available to do so, assign unused floor sections throughout the process for future expansion. If a future action is identified, dedicate a space for it.

You will gain an amount of flexibility in future layouts, if there are blocks of space quickly available.
j. Apply simulation or modeling programs to evaluate different options.

♦ ♦ ♦

G. Develop other options for the block layout phase, manage the evaluation of options, select a favorable layout and approve it

When you have created a good option, copy it and create other options.

An excellent way to evaluate the layout options is to involve the stake-holders, the people and functions who will live in the new layout. Layout options are ideally suited for visual analysis that all can understand. Many can stand around the table, contribute, and compare. Group input, especially by the stakeholders, is very effective in layout decisions.

As a practical matter, find a place where you can leave the layout and options on display, in a project room. In order to explore new options easily, spread the footprint drawing on a horizontal surface, and provide templates for the stakeholders to arrange,

You will be able quickly to create multiple layout options, and demonstrate different ways to approach the overall objectives of the project, to show graphically how the necessary operations would fit into the facility and would interact with each other.

It is possible to assemble a presentation on a computer screen, but in my opinion a group of prints on paper is a superior technique; spread options on the conference table or tape them to the walls, compare, combine the best features.

Review options with the stakeholders, and discuss, create new options immediately. Be prepared for other options to be suggested, so have blank plans at hand for new thoughts. Expect that the participants may not understand the benefits of layout planning, or which aspects are productive, so be prepared both to explain and to appreciate their suggestions.

Repeat the process until a decision is reached. This sequence can be used to review both block and detailed layout phases.

The following steps work well to develop ideas and to choose the most effective, both for block layouts and for detailed layouts.

1. Use the floor plan, a footprint, of the facility. Use a scale of 1/8" = one foot, or 1 to 100.

2. Prepare templates of <u>all of</u> the components of the final layout, to the same scale. It is far easier to erase lines on a piece of paper, than to relocate. Just as the old carpentry adage says, to "Measure twice and cut once", be sure to get it right first.

3. Gather the participants around a table. Place the plant footprint on the table, then all of the templates. Ask the participants to construct options, by placing the templates on the footprint in the most effective manner.

During the process, the leader may point out advantages and short-comings of layouts, so that the group may prepare them wisely.

4. Record each option, perhaps with a photograph, perhaps by taping the templates to the footprint and starting a new arrangement.

5. Recommend the favored option to the decision-maker for a final decision.

6. At some point, one or more layouts may be transferred to CAD.

One alternative is to prepare options on the CAD system, but this process will be slower and will lack the dynamic and symbiotic elements of a group effort.

♦ ♦ ♦

H. CAD drawing and model / simulation software

At this point let's talk about CAD drawing and model / simulation software. I will not rate them, because the state of the art moves quickly. Note that within AutoCad, and within Siemens, the drawing software is designed to interact with simulation software.

1. Commercial programs. The following are programs that are well received by practitioners in 2013. The quotes are from experienced practitioners, and the differences of opinion reflect their own use of the programs.

a. "The content of layout planning differs for the mechanical engineers and industrial engineers. AutoCAD, PDMS, Plant3D are very good for designing the infrastructure and architectural elements, however layout planning by definition is more about optimizing the material flows (logistics) which is very basically a function of distances and trip frequencies.

In that area AutoCAD, PDMS, Plant3D, etc., do not have the analysis and iterative optimization capabilities of Siemens PLM's Plant Design & Layout tools.

And of course Siemens' tools are not flexible enough to design the HVAC and piping like the other software's can do. You need to choose your tools according to the task at your hands."

b. Other say, "Siemens can perform HVAC and piping very well."

c. "FactoryCad, Flow and Plan embedded in AutoCad and part of Siemens PLM Suite is great with material handling analysis."

d. "AutoCAD and don't let anyone tell you different!"

2. Layout algorithms. Extended discussions of layout algorithms are available at several sources on line. The term "genetic algorithms" is also used. The "shortest path" of material flow is one key approach to optimize layouts, and function "adjacencies" (closeness) is another. Note that use of both may yield entirely different layouts.

3. Any layout, developed by a computer program or more manually, will depend on the quality of the assumptions and of the complicating factors inherent in the particular operation. The complicating factors are discussed throughout this book, but generally they relate to how many different products are included in a flow, volume and mix changes possible, lot size, future growth, building size and shape, space limitations, expansion possibilities, and the flexibility desired of all factors.

Layout itself with a computer program or a more manual analysis will require very careful definition of all the factors that limit flow in actual practice; walls, main aisles, the choice of equipment e. g. carts v conveyor, batch size, modular / cellular flow, changeover or other process interruption that causes extra in-process inventory, differential cycle time between processes involved.

◆ ◆ ◆

I. For detailed layout, within a department or function

Specific detailed layout positions equipment, machines, work stations, desks, tables, benches, conveyors, shelves, storage racks; all within the favored block layout plan approved earlier. Don't perform this step until the block plan is chosen.

1. Review the future expansion plan for a facility, and assure that the specific department layouts follow the plan to leave space throughout the layout for later use, or to set an expansion direction and leave it available until it is later used.

2. Early on, define immovable objects in the building; elevators, stairs, piping, air exhaust, rest rooms, load bearing walls. Position layout elements to interact with or to avoid.

3. Create a template set of the machines, work places, conveyors, racks, bins, storage and support items that will reside in the specific layout.

Print out the templates at the same scales as chosen for the building plans.
Create a template for everything that occupies floor space.

4. Use a Flow Chart to understand the process and material flow within the area of the specific layout. Absolutely resolve every step of the process.

First, identify potential improvement that has previously been discussed and put it into effect with the layout. Involve a wide participation of people and disciplines during the analysis.

Remember the steps in flow charting, and that 4 of the 5 are waste: Only "Operation" is productive; "Move", "delay", "inspect", and "store" are all waste.

But, be practical to recognize that inefficient practices may in fact occur. Provide space for planned and unplanned interruptions and delay in production. If possible, arrange equipment so that a production problem in one location does not stop production elsewhere, merely because of space.

5. Place equipment, workplaces, and staging on the footprint plan, to create shorter flow paths between equipment in the process.

Organize and cut through the "spaghetti" flow that adds distance and confusion. To the extent possible lay out operations as straight line or U shaped flow, within the department, to simplify handling and shorten distances between operations departments in the product flow.

Place work stations and inventory to amplify interactions of material and information flow with associated stations. Recognize preceding and following operations, as well as necessary support functions that interact. Relationships may be important, such as stations of a conveyor. They may possibly be irrelevant.

6. Place fixed equipment, for instance those with foundations or piping or air handling or waste treatment, so that it can remain in place at the time of a future expansion or re-layout. (Even if the resulting flow is not totally efficient.)

7. Use three dimensions; not only the floor but also mezzanines, upper stories, high rise racks. This practice reduces floor space, and can improve flow by vertical feeds, even to use gravity flow instead of powered movement.

Reserve high ceilings, and high load capacity floors, for equipment that requires them. Arrange tall equipment together if possible, so that ceiling heights can be kept low for initial and operating cost purposes.

8. Place equipment outside the facility walls; silos, tanks, hoppers can often hold bulk materials outside where they are accessible to supply vehicles, and don't use more valuable inside space.

9. Plan comprehensively for movement of raw materials, in-process, and finished products throughout the operation including the handling system, aisle widths, and access to production equipment.

Size storage areas according to the fundamental inventory control process employed in the facility; just in time, or just in case.

Allow access to machines for maintenance.

10. Understand the materials handling plan, and then place aisles, conveyors, work stations and staging accordingly.

For instance, if a conveyor is to be used, work stations will necessarily adjoin the conveyor, in a limited number of orientations. Determine the conveyor length by the size of the workstations, their material in-feeds, and materials flow. Place the conveyor grouping in the layout as a unit.

If material will be moved among workstations by carts or wheeled devices or by hand, individual workstations may be placed in any orientation. Provide space also for the transfer devices, staging, and materials flow.

In either event consider the relative time for each operation. In-process inventory, and space, may be reduced by tying successive operations closely together, but labor content will increase and output will decrease during any instance when one operation must wait on another.

11. What is the plan when one work station or department is idled? Do other sequential stations stop also? Or do they keep producing? If other stations keep producing, there must be room in the layout for that inventory, and for any storage equipment necessary. It is not unusual to provide space for a certain amount of inventory, for instance on an accumulating conveyor belt, to absorb minor interruptions without affecting other positions, but longer delays may shut them down.

12. Don't transfer materials just to transfer; move using the carrier that will be used in the work station. If another carrier is needed at the next workstation, place material into that carrier at the end of the previous operation.

13. Make product flow and inventory through the process visible. There are fewer surprises when inventory is visible to those who will use it, stockhandlers, and management.

14. Develop options by involving stakeholders for the detailed layout, just as in the block layouts. There will be a different group of stakeholders around the table, but arranging templates on a footprint is effective both ways.

♦ ♦ ♦

J. Three Dimensions, and Outside the Walls

Layout is typically two dimensional, but do not forget height.

Within the facility, assure that each equipment and workplace has enough room for its vertical dimension, and for access into it for operation or maintenance in all three dimensions.

1. Many buildings can effectively utilize multiple floors. An existing building, or a facility to be erected, may be multi-story. Layout considerations include two sides of the same coin; vertical flow can be very effective, yet materials handling may be difficult to arrange.

Vertical flow can be very effective. Usually from upstairs down, let gravity help. This is especially true where mixing is a first step for liquids, powers, or fluids followed by flow to the next operation. Gravity may allow flow without pumps. Other parts and subassemblies can utilize a vertical feed instead of horizontal via chutes, slides or dumbwaiters.

Materials handling may be difficult to arrange. Stairs and elevators are inconvenient. Floor load capacity and ceiling height may be limited.

2. Supplies can be located outside to good effect. Bulk materials which can be stored in bins, silos, hoppers, tanks may be kept outside the building. Not only raw materials but also waste products and perhaps in-process may be retained. Outside storage relieves demand for inside space, and filling and emptying the containers with over-the-road vehicles is often practical which alleviates dock traffic.

3. Do not forget that outside storage can block expansion of the facility in that area. Interior re-arrangement of products associated with that storage may also be more difficult.

◆ ◆ ◆

K. Tomorrow's plan: action now to catch up, then grow smoothly

Before you plan for the future, resolve today's issues first, then you can build the improvements into future plans. Understand what today's space issues and constraints are, and determine just what correction is needed now, and where, in order to meet today's sales volume efficiently.

For instance, when you implement any beneficial actions, use the results of the actions to establish a new baseline of space and output. Forecast growth and the space expansion based on changes.

◆ ◆ ◆

L. Show Stoppers

Are there potential problems which could seriously delay the project? Some possibilities which could extend the critical path include:

1. Insufficient inventory to allow the source to shut down.

2. Long lead time construction or permitting process necessary at the destination, such as:
    Paint, plate, chemical treatment, sand, anodize; exhaust or emission requirements.
    Heavily plumbed process, floor drains
    High ceilings requiring special steel members
    Material handling overhead cranes
    Weight requirements for floor or beams
    Hazardous waste for disposal
    Equipment mounted in pits, or heavy foundations
    Special air quality, temperature, pressure rooms
    Unusual power, water, gas, sewer requirements

3. Complex technology transfer including the people involved; and / or poor documentation

4. Incompatible electronics, hardware, or software between source and destination.

5. Overly optimistic learning curve assumed at the destination.

6. Change in computer hardware or software concurrently with move; arrange that computer changes be done before or after.

7. Not having to do with layout, allow for time and effort to plan and implement: permits, equipment commissioning, validation, certification, approval by internal, trade, state or federal regulatory entities.

◆ ◆ ◆

Chapter 19   Technology transfer, documentation

Topics in this chapter will apply to a technical operation, and may affect any layout of the equipment and personnel involved. Please consider these aspects, before and during development of layouts, especially if the layout is of technical or highly controlled processes, or if a subsequent relocation is large, or over a distance.

Generally speaking, the better the documentation, the less the challenge to relocate an operation over a distance.

Generally speaking, if the same operating people will be at the new destination, there is less challenge.

A. Product documentation may include

- Product and subassembly specifications, revision history
- Parts drawings and dimensions
- Bills of materials
- Routers
- Raw material requirements, indirect materials, commodities, and supplies; purchase specs
- Material usage standard and history
- Annual volume requirements
- Vendor list
- MSDS sheets
- Product packaging, primary and secondary, artwork and labels; specs, materials, vendors
- CAD-CAM drawings and electronic files; hardware and software to apply them with

◆ ◆ ◆

B. Process documentation may include
- Flow process, equipment layout
- Standardized and documented processes, procedures
- Machine settings; dimensions, pressure, feeds, temperature, speed, etc. Utilities provided and usage; input settings.
- Training manuals
- Operator instructions, Engineered methods for repeatability.
- Man / machine chart; right hand left hand chart, ergonomics work station design
- Work measurement; time study, Predetermined Times, Line balance

- Data library of allowed times for elements
- Process simulation
- Theory of constraints, Constraints management
- Operator training plan, learning curve
- Cycle times and batch sizes to meet customer demands and timing.
- Manning and crew sizes, nominal and actual output and productivity
- Videotape of key processes and operations.
- Computer Integrated Manufacturing electronic records
- Special environmental conditions

◆ ◆ ◆

C. Control and management documentation may include
- Standard Labor and Product Cost, Labor hours and crew
- Equipment depreciation status
- Output Records
- Schedules, work in process points and amounts, finished goods inventory levels,
- Reports of past performance; Volume, Cost, Schedule Attainment
- Capacity expectations and assumptions
- Plant, department learning curve information
- Overhead allocation

◆ ◆ ◆

D. Materials management documentation may include
- Vendor lists
- Scheduling of purchases and production to meet sales demands.
- Router, Schedules, Output Records,
- Actual inventory control, virtual / electronic / manual; inventory accuracy; any coding of location or production

◆ ◆ ◆

E. Quality documentation may include
- Quality standards, inspection criteria, reference samples throughout
- In process Quality control / feedback of problems
- Reports of quality history, deviations
- Lab results, physical, chemical, biological from beginning through current production
- ISO, Statistical process control, 6 Sigma, TQM or other files and records
- Calibration requirements, tools and gages used.

- Acceptability of components and product compared to specifications and customer needs; problems and solutions.
- Acceptable reclaim processes. Limit samples of components and product.
- Process validation documents
- Regulatory documents; history, submissions, approvals; status of pending

◆ ◆ ◆

F. Equipment documentation may include
- Operating equipment list
- Equipment records, for purchase, startup, operation, and process validation; historical operation and maintenance. Drawings and manuals. Warranty and service agreements, source of technical info and parts. CAD CAM, electronic files.
- Equipment set up instructions, maintenance manuals, changeover sequence
- Specialty tools, dies and fixtures for operation
- Spare parts, change parts, consumable parts; molds, inserts, heads. Tooling and fixtures.
- Preventive maintenance schedules, materials, and records. Calibration programs, demand maintenance record.
- Quick change capability, Single Minute Change of Die Capacity
- Materials handling and storage facilities and equipment.

◆ ◆ ◆

G. IT documentation may include
- Hardware and software necessary to administer operation and control; manuals and procedures
- Dialup, cable, DSL connections to the internet
- Up link / down link for satellite communications

◆ ◆ ◆

H. Factory Overhead documentation may include
- Organization chart
- Support organization: administration; scientists, engineers, and technical; production; finance and materials; quality assurance and human resources; sales and marketing; design and documentation.

◆ ◆ ◆

Chapter 20   The destination; prepare it

A destination may today be in use for another purpose, or vacant. As part of the layout process, first plan not how the new occupants will fit in, but what is necessary to vacate and prepare the area for occupancy. If the area is now occupied that obviously involves a more complex situation.

To initiate the destination layout, first determine the physical characteristics of all portions of the area. Then define the requirements of the incoming operation, and make modifications at the destination that are necessary.

Checkerboard moves are common, in which one occupant is moved to another location as step one, and subsequent steps relocate successive occupants. In such a sequence, the destination preparation is repeated.

"Ownership" can be a concern, but is not addressed here. See chapter 51 "Ownership" for further guidance.

Section F addresses the normal processes for assuring that a property meets the occupancy requirements, and the occasional circumstances to meet internal or external regulatory requirements.

A. Determine the physical characteristics of the destination.

1. Physical characteristics include capacities and limitations: dimensions, shape, condition, lighting, temperature, humidity; floor composition, floor load capacity, clear height, dock, elevators, materials access.

Consider suitability for manufacturing, process, storage, support, and administrative areas. capability for expansion.

2. Incoming Utility Capacity
   a.   Electricity, KWH; 110v, 220v, 220v 3 phase, 440v 3 phase

   b.   Water, gallons; Hot, Cold, Chilled, Deionized, Sterile,

   c.   Gases, piped

   d.   Process Steam, capacity

e. High Pressure Air

3. Telecommunications; Telephone, computer connections

4. Security system, cameras, monitors, entrances, guard locations

5. Waste disposal capacity
   a. Drains, where and capacity

   b. Chemical drains, where and capacity

   c. Exhaust fans location and capacity, both to the atmosphere and to hazardous materials collection.

6. Facility requirements to satisfy operations and support functions
If the destination is not in the same building or on the same campus, these factors should be considered.

   a. Parking spaces

   b. Grounds fenced? Entry gate?

   c. Employee entrances, time clocks

   d. Reception and visitors facilities

   e. Hiring and training

   f. Meeting, conference rooms

   g. Cafeteria and break areas; in-house or contract equipment, services. Vending machines or food preparation? Future change?

   h. Rest rooms, locker rooms, Employee store

   i. Provisions for day care on site, now or future

   j. Medical care facility, staffed or contract

   k. Truck Docks
            Product Out, In
            Product waste, recycle out; dedicated garbage dock, dumpsters
            Trucker waiting / rest room / dispatcher

l. Dock height

m. Dock door height, width

n. Rail, barge connections

o. Silos, bulk storage

p. Apron size / parked trailers

q. Outdoor storage

B. Compare the destination to the requirements of the incoming operation.

1. Use the same criteria as listed above, to define the requirements of the incoming operation. Even if the same connections exist, such as for utilities, confirm that the necessary quantities can be provided.

2. Consider and arrange to handle, all kinds of waste created; permits and handlers.
    a. Expected monthly generation of solid waste which may be recycled

    b. Expected monthly generation of solid waste which may not be recycled

    c. Expected monthly generation of liquid waste

3. Sanitary, Chemical, Process, Storm rains

4. Expected monthly generation of airborne waste, by category

Quantify any shortcomings of the destination, and define how to deal with them.

◆ ◆ ◆

C. Lay out the destination

1. Fit the incoming operation into the destination, with a block layout. After approval of the chosen one, prepare a detailed layout, accurate enough to locate each piece of equipment and furnishing, and all utility connections.

2. Determine what construction or modification is necessary. Walls, partitions, services, drains, HVAC. Environmental areas, fire protection.

3. Establish a budget for physical changes needed. Judge which physical changes are mandatory to accomplish the layout and which would be very helpful; prioritize them. Make cost estimates for each line item, and add them up. What cannot be done? Is it possible to operate without these features? If not, go back for more money.

4. When a budget is set and approved, freeze the layout and do not allow further changes. Publish the complete layout with connections. Obtain signed approval for the final layouts.

◆ ◆ ◆

D. Modify the destination to the incoming operation

1. Prepare purchase orders for construction or modification.

2. Ask for construction bids. Let them according to company policy.

3. Obtain permits and approvals.

4. Take possession of the new facility as soon as possible to check out the mechanical issues; keys fit, power is on, air conditioning works, phones are connected, toilets flush, carpets are cleaned.

5. Construct and modify the destination.

◆ ◆ ◆

E. Prepare the modified destination for occupancy

1. Physically mark the destination with locations for power, phones, computer connections. Mark locations for equipment and furnishings, and connections for other utilities.

2. Run power, phones, computer lines. Run utility lines and drops to each piece of equipment.

3. Mark aisles, post signs and labels.

4. Run communications and computers in parallel in advance of the move if possible. If not possible, test all lines.

◆ ◆ ◆

F. Assure that a property meets occupancy and regulatory requirements.

1. Normal occupancy requirements include such as proper electrical voltage, light levels for specific tasks, water pressure, system check-out of equipment such as boilers, HVAC, motor centers, telephones, computer wiring, et al; culminating with the items on the certificate of occupancy from local building inspectors. Software for facility operation and security must also be properly validated in place.

2. Internal or external regulatory requirements.
For local building codes, emergency lighting, sprinkler systems, elevators.

For external certification, facility and equipment and process validations with documentation, such as ISO standards.

FDA, food preparation or USDA approvals if needed will extend through extensive on-site inspections before approval. Even a change in a manufacturing sourcing for some products can require approval. Such approvals will typically constitute a substantial part of the critical path schedule.

Equipment installation and commissioning is the final step for major purchase orders of equipment, before a vendor turns over equipment.

◆ ◆ ◆

Chapter 21   Pack and move

This chapter concerns the detailed actions to perform the culmination of a relocation, the pack and move itself.

A. Assumptions

People and equipment are at point A, the source.
People and equipment are to be at point B, the destination.

◆ ◆ ◆

B. Understand the plan

See the existing plan and understand it especially objectives, scope, dates, responsibilities, layouts, contracts let, transition as it affects employees and clients, communications to date.

◆ ◆ ◆

C. Timing

What are the key dates? Are they set in concrete? Even if they are mandated without considering the work involved, build them into the plans to see if it is practical to meet them. Appeal the dates only after you have a grasp of the costs of achieving them and the consequences of revising them.

Create a master calendar, starting with the move date. Calculate other major dates from the move date. Be sure to include dates for upcoming holidays and vacations. Critical dates can include
1. Computer off at source, computer on at destination
2. Phones off at source, phones on at destination
3. Take possession of destination
4. General preparation starts
5. Final packing starts
6. Moving truck appears at source, departs source, arrives at destination, departs.
7. Unpack to get operation going starts, is done
8. Operation is back to normal

◆ ◆ ◆

D. Notify customers and employees

1. Transition
   Pick a transition time and publicize it to clients, customers, vendors, shippers, utilities, employees. If possible make the transition over a weekend or long weekend.

2. Employees
   Ask / require employees to work during the transition especially to pack and unpack their own workplace.

◆ ◆ ◆

E. Riggers and movers

1. Ask qualified riggers and movers to visit and quote on equipment, furniture, and furnishings that is beyond the company capability to move. Review quotes and check references of the favored companies. Understand the insurance available, costs and coverage, and thoughtfully select and confirm a plan in writing.

2. Award the contracts and negotiate dates and timing. Determine if the rigger will disconnect and reconnect utilities or company people will do so. Identify the safety regulations riggers and movers will be required to follow. Appoint a member of the plant team to direct the riggers and movers.

3. At the time production is shut down allow the riggers access, and monitor their work and progress.

◆ ◆ ◆

F. Moving Insurance

You will face the question of insurance for the equipment that you relocate while it is the mover's responsibility. There is no one constant answer, yes you should insure or no, you needn't. Nor will you have a firm idea of the dollar limits of the policy. The cost will be higher than you think is necessary, and you will consider the possibility of a problem to be slight.

But you must balance the cost and likelihood of loss against the size of the risk and the damage to your business if a moving van were to be in an accident, or a computer CPU dropped.

◆ ◆ ◆

G. Security

Moves are not business as usual, and otherwise rigid security rules may be relaxed unintentionally. Be sure to protect the confidential aspects and intellectual property of the business during a move, as well as the physical assets.

◆ ◆ ◆

H. Pack

1. Preparation
   a. Make a layout for the existing facility and all furnishings, furniture and equipment.
   b. Assign an identification number to all work areas and all furnishings, furniture and equipment on the layout. Post drawings and lists in conspicuous places throughout the facility. Label each work area and all furnishings, furniture and equipment with a visible colored tape.
   c. Define "Pack Up". Are file drawers to be emptied? Desk drawers? Bookcases and shelves and desktops? Presumably "Pack Up" means to place into moving boxes the contents which must be confined before equipment is relocated.
   d. Are some furnishings, furniture and equipment not to be placed in the main new facility? If so color code them differently on layouts and individual markings. Define what is to happen, whether move off and leave, or stage somewhere.
   e. Assign to specific individual employees the responsibility to "pack up" and later unpack each work area and all furnishings, furniture and equipment. Record and publish the assignments
   f. Publish guidelines for packing; weight limits, protection from damage, tape application, marking of contents, color coding.

2. Pre-pack
   a. Buy enough packing cartons for all material to be relocated, with plenty of extra.
   b. Issue a supply of cartons to each employee who has a packing responsibility, and stage the surplus in convenient spots.
   c. Provide marking pens, color coded tape, sealing tape and tape applicators.
   d. The responsible employees can, in advance, pack items not critical to operations such as photos, wall hangings, file archives.
   e. Technicians create a connection plan for each electrical and electronic device, defining all cords and cable schemes.

3. Packing day Facility does not do business this day.
a. Pack
    1. The responsible employees pack items that are critical to operations, then tape the carton shut, then mark and color code the carton.
    2. The responsible employees confirm that all furnishings, furniture and equipment are labeled with identification and destination codes.
    3. The responsible employees confirm that all packed cartons are labeled with identification and destination codes and that there are no unmarked objects.
    4. Employees leave.

b. Disconnect
More or less simultaneously but without interference, technicians disconnect electrical and electronic equipment. Unplug electrical cords, cables, peripheral equipment. Mark equipment, cords and cables for correct reconnection. Tape cords and cables to the equipment they serve.
    1. Telephones
    2. Computers
    3. Electrical equipment.

◆ ◆ ◆

I. Move

Movers come in and remove furnishings, furniture, equipment and packed boxes from the origin. Place furnishings, furniture, equipment at the specific location called for on the layouts. Place packed boxes in the specific areas of the layouts.
    Riggers move equipment.

◆ ◆ ◆

J. Unpack

1. Unpack
a. The responsible employees unpack items that are critical to operations and put them in their proper place so that operations can be resumed.
b. The responsible employees can at the appropriate time unpack items not critical to operations.

2. Reconnect

Technicians reconnect electrical and electronic equipment. Plug in electrical cords, cables, peripheral equipment using marked equipment, cords and cables. Turn on equipment and verify that it operated and is correctly connected.

a. Telephones
b. Computers
c. Electrical equipment.
d. Technicians remain on call for problems.

Riggers or employees place and reconnect equipment and operate it to assure it is in working order, undamaged by the move.

◆ ◆ ◆

K. Recommence operations.

Place trained operators at qualified equipment, with appropriate documentation and approved materials. Start operations. Increase output according to predetermined learning curve expectations.

◆ ◆ ◆

Chapter 22   Master plan a facility

A facility master plan layout is the arrangement of all of the components required for a business to perform its charter. It is the broad view of design, layout, and the arrangement of people, materials and machines.

Master planning may be tailored to a property, to a building, or to an entire campus, depending on an organization's objectives.

Chapter 73 addresses master planning for a campus, and this chapter addresses a smaller property.

The Block Layout Concept, as described in Chapter 47, will provide the most useful approach to master planning.

The block layout determines the overall dimensions of an group of activities or department and draws them as one piece, a "block" of floor space. A block layout is very useful to evaluate, and to differentiate, general arrangement options within a building. It will allow flow planning between groups or functions. It will also make sure that all pieces of the operation will fit into the chosen area in the first place.

Block layout provides a visual aid to compare how different arrangements would provide for production efficiencies, flow, space utilization, growth, access. A block layout before final selection can also point out necessary building or property improvements and modification.

◆ ◆ ◆

A. Summary
Two tenets keep reappearing during effective master planning:

Plan for the present without blocking future options, and

Create smooth flow patterns for present day operations.

Neither is as easily done as said, but both can be accomplished with care.

First, "the layout". We speak of it as an entity, fixed in space and time but it really isn't. We will generate an initial layout which will evolve and grow and change over time. That is normal, nothing to fear.

If we are careful, that is. We will want to envision a master plan, and position the first layout phase for day one on the property so that we don't block future growth on the site. One building or several? We don't need to know that on day one. Build it all at once? You won't need to, just build each phase in such a way that we can add on the next building phase without difficulty and that can be done. However if you want to construct more than you need in the short term, it may be a useful option and may even be cost effective if you anticipate greater costs in the future, or more restrictive zoning.

Space usage in the short term may be quite different than the long term. Again, initial layout must not block future modifications, even if future plans are not totally clear.

◆ ◆ ◆

B. Keys to a successful Master Plan

There are quite a few factors than can be considered key to success, and they are considered below. Some will be more important than others in the particular project, and you will need to investigate the situation and prioritize in order to determine relative importance.

There is no particular ranking of the factors here; you'll have to decide based on the project circumstances.

1. To what extent you will make parts on site, or buy them. The more that are built on the site, the more manufacturing space but the less storage space is required.

2. Will there be dedicated sections to build components? Is the intention to place other industry, your sub-assembly vendors, on the site? These could modify the allocations.

3. Typically a new entity will buy more parts and assemblies early, with a plan to vertically integrate later and perform more work on site.

4. Space usage in the short and long terms may be quite different.

5. Are there features that must be added, employee amenities? Power plant or boilers or water treatment or waste disposal? Food service, day care, dormitories, prayer rooms?

6. The third dimension; will the facility be more than one story? The product may determine that; or the relative sizes of the property compared to the building; or the process.

♦ ♦ ♦

C. Place the overall facility on the property

Objective: Don't block the future usage by initial placements.

On the property, are there hills / valleys / water / low land that will be expensive to utilize? How to avoid them without affecting operations?

Can buildings be placed to avoid moving earth? Earth moving is expensive and usually does not add value.

Where are roads, rail, water, for incoming materials and outgoing product? Position the in and out docks very early in a convenient location where they do not later interfere with expansion on the property.

Does property require that buildings be long and slender, square shaped, ells, etc.

None of this is a problem, but there will be only one chance to plan the best fit, and that is day one.

♦ ♦ ♦

D. Plan for growth, and the relationships of multiple operations

Objective: Don't block the future usage by initial placements. But as well as the crystal ball permits, create a final plan to use space effectively and provide efficient flow patterns for all operations and components.

It is not a problem to build for a product and later to add similar lines for other products and / or volume. Try to anticipate growth and leave room in the master plan to do so.

The same is true for vertical integration; you may purchase parts initially, with a plan for a facility to make the component in-house in future years. Be sure to leave an empty location in the master plan to do so.

Are there any planned other products, that should have a spot reserved?

In the master layout we can specify a site even if it is not clear what is to occupy it in future years. Process flow may turn out to be inconvenient, but the master plan should provide avenues for materials handling and future technology, even without detail.

Create a master plan to deal with future product or technology changes.

♦ ♦ ♦

E. Characteristics of production, storage, admin buildings

The building designs will be different for production, admin, storage.
1. Storage is best suited for single floor, high ceilings, and attention to floor loads. A good planning system to avoid the need to have material on hand is far cheaper that buying and storing.

2. Production may require high ceilings in some areas but not throughout. Some machines may require heavy foundations, or strong building columns for overhead cranes. Try to distribute power, air, piping even drains overhead and not buried in concrete floors.

3. Administration functions well in multistory buildings, which may be cheaper per square foot than single floor and will use less space on the site. I do prefer for manufacturing and materials offices to be near their area of responsibility. Overall admin, engineering, finance, can be central.

♦ ♦ ♦

F. Flow within the overall layout

Can be straight line, U shaped, right angles.

In a large facility, flow within a dedicated area such as an integrated production line will be more important than flow between buildings or models.

An early department can have a certain capacity, but allow room for growth for greater capacity in the future if it can be forecast.

♦ ♦ ♦

G. Operating assumptions that will affect the layout

An important assumption is the kind of material planning and flow. Will the plant use just-in-time, where material is scheduled to show up just as it is needed? Without JIT, you will require a buffer stock which requires space on the layout. The layout must provide space for receiving, staging, inspection, storing, picking and issuing to production; for subassembly and in-process movement and staging to the next operations unless assembly lines are very carefully coordinated. The bottom line is that JIT takes less space and inventory cost, but can be risky if vendors let you down.

◆ ◆ ◆

H. Shared work stations or sub-assembly lines

Product models can share expensive or fixed facilities. Sharing raises the output level of the equipment, and create a broader base for justification, using quality and automation reasons. But sharing will tend to increase changeover, handling and cycle time, as distances will increase and scheduling interference may occur.

◆ ◆ ◆

I. Make / buy over time

To start up most quickly, and with the simplest, smallest layouts, plan to use components which are on the market, readily available, from one or more a reliable quality-conscious vendors, preferably nearby.

Then, justify vertical integration on a case-by-case basis if your plant can do the work as well, and less expensively.

◆ ◆ ◆

J. A sequence of events may occur over time to create a campus

1. Assemble a prototype, on a line or in an area. Refine bill of material and router.

2. Sketch out an assembly line with early make / buy plans. Design for full sized, mature line, with all final vertical integration.

3. Build a facility for the final assembly line, which early will have much available space because are buying many components.

4. Start assembly, buying some making some, relatively low line speed

5. Justify and add equipment for vertical integration, speed up flow

6. Reach a mature line, full speed, with final vertical integration.

◆ ◆ ◆

K. Expectations
Last, but this might have been first. The plant will meet management expectations. All the way through this project, everyone involved needs to understand just what is expected.

◆ ◆ ◆

Chapter 23   Workplace layout

Workplace layout is the arrangement of the tools, equipment, and materials that are present at a work station, as they relate to crew members and methods.

Frederick Taylor understood the importance of workplace layout, as did Frank and Lillian Gilbreath and other practitioners of classic industrial engineering. Who am I to improve on the original "Principles of Motion Economy" by Frank Gilbreath, whose basis goes back 125 years.

A. Use of the Human Body
1. The two hands should begin as well as complete their motions at the same time.

2. The two hands should not be idle at the same time except during rest periods.

3. Motions of the arms should be made in opposite and symmetrical directions and should be made simultaneously.

4. Hand motions should be confined to the lowest classification with which it is possible to perform the work satisfactorily.

5. Momentum should be employed to assist the worker wherever possible, and it should be reduced to a minimum if it must be overcome by muscular effort.

6. Smooth continuous motions of the hands are preferable to zigzag motions or straight-line motions involving sudden and sharp changes in direction.

7. Ballistic movements are faster, easier, and more accurate than restricted (fixation) or "controlled" movements.

8. Rhythm is essential to the smooth and automatic performance of an operation, and the work should be arranged to permit easy and natural rhythm wherever possible.

♦ ♦ ♦

B. Arrangement of the Work Place
  9. There should be definite and fixed place for all tools and materials.

10. Tools, materials, and controls should be located close to and directly in front of the operator.

11. Gravity feed bins and containers should be used to deliver material close to the point of use.

12. Drop deliveries should be used wherever possible.

13. Materials and tools should be located to permit the best sequence of motions.

14. Provisions should be made for adequate conditions for seeing. Good illumination is the first requirement for satisfactory visual perception.

15. The height of the work place and the chair should preferably be arranged so that alternate sitting and standing at work are easily possible.

16. A chair of the type and height to permit good posture should be provided for every worker.

◆ ◆ ◆

C. Design of Tools and Equipment

17. The hands should be relieved of all work that can be done more advantageously by a jig, a fixture, or a foot-operated device.

18. Two or more tools should be combined wherever possible.

19. Tools and materials should be pre-positioned whenever possible.

20. Where each finger performs some specific movement, such as in typewriting, the load should be distributed in accordance with the inherent capacities of the fingers.

21. Handles such as those used on cranks and large screwdrivers should be designed to permit as much of the surface of the hand to come in contact with the handle as possible. This is particularly true when considerable force is exerted in using the handle. For light assembly work the screwdriver handle should be so shaped that it is smaller at the bottom than at the top.

22. Levers, crossbars, and hand wheels should be located in such positions that the operator can manipulate them with the least change in body position and with the greatest mechanical advantage.

Chapter 24   Office move, a special case

An office move or rearrangement is similar to most other moves, but it tends to be a special case because of the personalities involved. The space assignments to executives and long-time employees who have the boss's ear, relative office size, a view, the customer interface that may occur, all warrant a high level of attention. Plus, because an office is often closely tied to customers, business interruption must be carefully controlled.

Office employees will often want to participate in their layout planning, so use their knowledge to benefit the results.

This chapter, a summary of points to be considered, should be routine factors in layout with the possible exception of the computer and phones. Essentially all of it is logistical in nature, applied to human relationships.

A. The plan

As in other facility actions, set the plan, prepare to implement it, then put the plan into effect.

◆ ◆ ◆

B. Set in concrete

Find out quickly from management what is decided and what is yet to be resolved. You may review the "decided" for egregious errors, but study the issue quietly until you identify and quantify all of the pertinent factors. Discuss if you will, then move on. Quickly get into the unresolved issues.

◆ ◆ ◆

C. Scope

Typically there will be
1. A general plan; such as "move from here to there January 13".
2. Several supporting plans; involving perhaps existing facility, destination facility, the move itself, support contract services, customer service, computer and telephone.

◆ ◆ ◆

D. Involvement of employees

Keep all those involved in the information loop, and react to problems quickly and fairly.

Communication is important in any layout and move, but more so when an office is the subject. The person doing the layout will automatically be the center, as people will drop in to see where they will sit in the new location, and they will offer suggestions. While this may provide a distraction, it also offers an opportunity to solicit suggestions and feedback and pass on information. Information flow must continue through the move itself, and the office inhabitants can be very useful to implement a successful move.

Relationships of people and functions are as important in offices as in a factory. Place departments and people near those they do business with. Allow employees a say in layouts to the extent possible, such as relationships that affect proximity of work stations.

Other primary factors in offices are floor space allowed and furnishings. Both are often called out in a company policy based on place in the organization, or rank. Sometimes relationships are tied to function; hiring and purchasing constantly interview outsiders and so need a larger office near an entrance door.

Seek guidance often from the management members of the area concerned. Give them opportunity to contribute, and certainly to approve the layouts as they progress.

When the move is scheduled, be sure to involve the people affected in the timing and the move itself. It is useful to appoint "captains" to represent a group, pass down information, answer questions or get them answered. Captains see that actions are done in their area, such as packing personal effects, desk drawers and files. It is usually a good idea to have each office member pack his or her individual office area, then later unpack it. Have those involved work on common areas.

◆ ◆ ◆

E. Assumptions and corollaries

Will the business be open during normal hours during the move?

Is the business computer-dependent? Yes means that the computer relocation will be the critical path. Assume that is true until proven otherwise.

What written plans or assignments have been made? What layouts agreed to? What contracts have been let already, bids submitted, brothers-in-law contacted?

Will some equipment not be moved because upgrades or replacements will be used at the destination? That will mean a different action set for such equipment.

Is there a floor layout of the existing facility? Of the new facility? An accurate inventory of equipment? Do not assume they are correct, at your peril.

Is there a new phone number or is the other one relocated? In either case you are dependent on the phone company and that is scary. Keep the phone company under your personal oversight and on a short leash. The best bet is to have the new phones installed and operating in the new facility in advance. That is easy if the phone number is new. You will be told it is impossible if the number is the same but challenge the phone company as high up as you can get to make it happen, perhaps as a separate set of extensions. Make them innovate. If they insist on a change the day of the move, called a cutover, check their plans and backups and performance closely.

◆ ◆ ◆

F. Timing

What are the key dates? Are they set in concrete? Even if they are mandated without considering the tasks involved, build them into the plans to see if it is practical to meet them. Appeal the dates only after you have a grasp of the costs of achieving them and the consequences of revising them. Include upcoming holidays and vacations.

Create a master calendar, starting with the move date. Calculate other major dates from the move date. In this case, critical dates can include
Computer off at source, computer on at destination
Phones off at source, phones on at destination
Take possession of destination, start modifications; another date for when they are done.
General preparation for the move starts within the office
Final packing starts
Moving truck appears at source, departs source, arrives at destination, departs.
Unpack at destination starts; is done
Operation is back to normal

◆ ◆ ◆

G. Action plans including assignments and timetables.

Creating and updating plans will be a continuing activity until the day of the move. Start with a series of "To Do" lists. Assign responsibility for each task; you have to do this before setting a viable timetable because Mary Lou may have 24 hours of work and you only allow her 8 hours. Manipulate the "to do" and assignments within the time allowed.

After you have created a series of lists of necessary activities, formally assign them and the due dates.

♦ ♦ ♦

H. Pre-occupancy

Take possession of the destination as soon as possible to allow you to check out the mechanical issues in advance; keys fit, power is on, air conditioning works, phones are connected, toilets flush, carpets are cleaned, resolve building sharing issues.

♦ ♦ ♦

Chapter 25   A jam-packed building and how to cope

Congested facilities can cost efficiency and reaction time, decrease safety, and damage product; both management and employees dislike the situation. This chapter suggests actions to correct a space deficit <u>right now</u>, even though your crystal ball may not be perfectly clear to prepare for the future, and even if you choose to be selective with expenditures.

Consider your space issues in four dimensions; not only the three dimensions of your facilities but also the fourth dimension, time. If possible determine the final, long term space plan and construct the short term fix so that it fits into the long term solution.

A. Today's crunch

When you deal with a space crunch, day-to-day and long term may be intertwined, for both problems and solutions.

A long term space solution may be clear, to build or add on. But construction will take time, and may in fact cause more congestion in the very area that is in need of relief today. To the extent possible, consider long term solutions first and fit in short term solutions that augment, or at least do not interfere, with the long term.

These ideas have proved useful in the past so consider them for your situation, for the geometry and flow of your facilities.

1. Solve your long term space problem with a checker game; move something so you can move something else, and start a progression that will result, in time, with the favored configuration.

<u>The key requirement for a checker game is to have one open square.</u>

But if you have a space problem today, presumably you do not have many open squares. The apparent answer then is to create an open area to accommodate the first relocation, then make the first of several moves.

2. One very useful practice is to create an open square on your checker table by constructing the first part of the long term solution. Then move into that, preferably with the detailed layout which will fit into the final arrangement. A recent client had the opportunity to "square off" a building, adding sections in two directions and enough area

to allow the checker-board moves that would alleviate space constraints in most operating departments.

3. Clear out an empty space through a basic change in procedures which can be inexpensive but require an entirely new approach; clean out obsolete inventory; move into a formal Just in Time inventory program with vendors and minimize internal inventories. Prevail on vendors to delay delivery, ask buyers to take delivery early. Use a local distribution firm to store finished goods as well as ship them for you. (This might be especially useful if a few large customers occupy a significant amount of your finished goods inventory.) Even place this fulfillment service in another region of the country to cut delivery time there and increase customer service.

4. Create an empty spot by leasing an outside facility to store material now in the on-site warehouse, use the warehouse space to ease congestion. Better yet, reduce your inventories to free up warehouse space.

5. Facility rentals are of course a common option to generate the first open area. It may even be possible in your area to use temporary facilities such as tobacco warehouses or fruit and vegetable warehouses which are empty until the next growing season.

6. Use corporate facilities elsewhere, put up a temporary building on your premises.

7. Add facilities, if there is a solid and incremental sales growth projection. Consider a location adjoining, or nearby, or remote to fit into geographic market objectives.

8. The classic expedient used universally is to store materials temporarily in semi-trailers, at a dock or parked. This can be an excellent idea, or not so good. The "excellent" technique is to unload raw materials directly from a trailer into production, just in time at its most efficient. Then, load finished goods directly into trailers for shipment to the customer.

Using trailers as a mini-warehouse usually results in horrible space utilization if an aisle is needed for access to material; if the trailer can be unloaded from its door back, over time, the result may be acceptable.

9. Your operation might be able to use a specialized change in procedures, switch from pallet loads of material to bulk storage. If you now buy materials on pallets, consider bulk that can be stored in tanks or silos or hoppers. If you do this, be sure to position tanks or silos so that they don't block future expansion.

10. Do you concurrently have a space crunch and overcapacity? The worst of all worlds, but not uncommon in today's economy. The crunch can occur because there is on hand too much of the wrong thing, considering sales; perhaps equipment or inventory of a slow moving product. If the organization is willing to phase out the product or service, the space decision follows easily; dispose of surplus. Even if the decision is to keep the product or service, space issues can be relieved by the actions above.

◆ ◆ ◆

B. Tomorrow's Plan: a step function now to catch up, then grow smoothly

Understand what today's space issues and constraints are, and determine just what correction is needed now, and where, in order to meet sales volume efficiently. Implement this "step function" first to create a real base line in two parts. 1) Establish and define the sales level and product mix. 2) Assign adequate space to each entity of the organization to fulfill its mission at the defined volume and mix.

Then forecast growth and the expansion necessary to meet it, predicated on an efficient operation even if you may not have one today. Plan long term growth after the step function is completed; forecast sales increases and convert them to the floor space needed, recognizing short term corrections that you've made.

Space planning is always dependent on product mix. If possible forecast the future volume to recognize general variation between today and future product mix.

◆ ◆ ◆

Chapter 26   Relocation to an existing company facility

Often a move is planned into an existing company facility, for strategic or timing reasons. It is usually expected that such a move is easier, simpler. This may well be true, but be alert for potential issues. Ask these questions to gain insights.

A. In this section, a "no" answer can signal an issue.

1. a) Are processes defined, documented, and operating to the extent desired now?
   b) To the extent required to relocate?

2. Are there similar processes in the destination facility?

3. Will the people who now operated the process relocate?
   a) Technical
   b) Supervisory
   c) Hourly

4. Will processes be moved as is? If changes will be made simultaneously. Watch out.

5. a) Is a computerized plant layout available in both location?
   b) Are plant layouts current?

6. Is computer simulation capability available?

7. Is there space available in the destination now?

8. Are both the operation to be moved, and the destination, free of environmental hazards?

♦ ♦ ♦

B. In this section, the higher the answer, the greater the difficulty

1. How many steps or phases in the move process?

2. How many major pieces of equipment are involved?

3. a) How many square feet in the origin plant?

b) In the destination?

4. About how many independent operations to relocate?

5. About how many people?

◆ ◆ ◆

C. For this section, there is no "right" or "wrong" answer, but consider the ramifications of the question in your circumstances

1. How large is the time window when equipment may be out of operation?

2. Do materials flow from point to point on a conveyor, or in a batch mode?

3. Will the relocation be all at once or sequential over time?

4. How many employees will be dedicated to the project?
   a. Origin facility
   b. Destination facility

5. Will dismantling, rigging, shipping, installation be done in house or contracted?

6. Will destination site preparation be done in-house or subcontracted?

◆ ◆ ◆

Chapter 27   Layout for the truly expert

While much layout can be well performed by those with limited skills, there are a few categories that demand a real expert. Much layout involves a precision only that a cabinet drawer doesn't hit a desk but other tasks demand more precision.

Some layout requires an exact alignment of screw holes for equipment that will be fastened together; this is layout science reserved for the truly well qualified. Pipe layouts for a refinery demand a skill most of us can hardly imagine.

A systems integrator will lay out for instance a highly mechanized combination of conveyors, machines, feeds, transfers, take offs, gates, stops, and actuators. This technical layout is for the skilled.

The objective of most projects is actually several layouts, options, for the client to pick and choose, probably to ask for further revision, to take this option but add the features from that arrangement, and finally to have a hybrid that provides the most effective result. Layouts will usually involve some compromise. While there is nothing written in stone that says a perfect layout is impossible, in practice the best option will have some very good points but some flaws as well, that can't be resolved without a worse problem.

Layouts may even be one project that a committee can perform well. I remember an office layout that I strove mightily over, wasn't crazy about it but it was the best I could come up with. The people who would work in the office were not too keen on it either. One lady enquired, what if we turn the desks to face west rather than north? Well, I hastened to point out that a desk space is about square, and there would be no improvement. Can you try it she asked. Sure, but it won't make any difference. So I turned the desk templates, while all watched, and the furnishings fit like a hand in a glove. And since the occupants were able to make a contribution to this near perfect fit, all were pleased.

There is no way to predict how the geometry of the facility and of the furnishings will interact. One example that is easy to understand is a simple parking lot. You will want an access lane and one or two rows of parking spaces, right? If the lot dimensions are wide enough, a center lane and spaces at right angles will fit. If the width is narrower, use a center lane and two rows of angled spaces. Even narrower, a lane and two rows of spaces for parallel parking; narrower still and one lane, only one row of spaces. Your building dimensions will dictate just how the equipment and furnishings and access aisles can be arranged.

<u>After all, what is a good layout for?</u>

A good layout will simultaneously consider an organization's business model and inventory control practices; operating processes, equipment and furnishings; inter-functional proximity relationships; operating space requirements by equipment; output demand; capacity and utilization by constraint; cycle time objectives, detailed product flow through the process; incoming, outgoing and in-process material storage; floor load limits and ceiling limitations, building, material handling and equipment dimensions; and future growth intentions. At least.

That is why layout is not just about fitting workstations into a building floor plan, because no two facilities or processes are the same. There will not be a template on the web, or a standard floor plan, that matches your situation. Or one book either, come to think of it.

You will see that the relationships above are not always linear, that is from point to point. Usually they are circular; reach a resolution in one place and that revises an input you considered earlier. Layout is an iterative process, and the result gets better as you progress.

Will you know when you have it right? Probably not. Is there a better plan, which a more skilled practitioner would develop? Maybe, maybe not. Good luck.

◆ ◆ ◆

Chapter 28   Layout during facility consolidation

An organization's strategy may be to consolidate processes, facilities and equipment, from multiple organizations or entities. The objective is typically to create an integrated, effective, productive enterprise which maximizes operating and distribution synergies from the previous individual elements.

Issues other than layout abound as well in a consolidation. Chapter 77 in the following section deals with these issues.

This chapter addresses layout, because its success contributes to the effectiveness of the consolidation.

◆ ◆ ◆

A. What is to be in the new layout?

This question is always one of the first to be asked, usually one of the last to be answered in a consolidation. Consolidations involve multiple facilities, multiple management structures, usually several options and the choices can be difficult. And the decisions are often made at levels above the layout planner.

Keep the current list of equipment front and center. Identify each layout variation with the equipment assumptions clearly. Expect that assumptions will change.

Equipment will typically be that which is most useful to meet output, quality, product mix and cost objectives in the final configuration. A consolidated layout may include similar or identical equipment, or completely dissimilar, or new process technology to be added during the consolidation.

Equipment which could become useful as future volume or product mix changes may be retained, in the layout or in storage.

A complicating factor in consolidations is that the layout personnel are often not familiar with one or more processes, or sets of equipment. Technology transfer practices and information flow can delay the planned process.

◆ ◆ ◆

B. Consolidation attributes

The processes being consolidated may have had different inventory models, both JIT and Just in Case, for instance. Understand the plan for the final configuration and position material stores accordingly.

Consider any new management control or planning system to be implemented during the consolidation.

Layout manufacturing and process, storage, support, and administrative areas.

◆ ◆ ◆

C. Integrate operations of companies involved

Consider these factors during layout:

1. Is the plan to separate or integrate the departments being arranged?

2. Are equipment lines to be dedicated to a product, or flexible?

3. Sharing of common areas and facilities; e. g. docks.

4. Sharing of supervision, support and administration

5. As in any layout, consider process flow; capacity of production equipment; capability of equipment to produce different product models and styles; capacity of materials handling and storage facilities and equipment.

6. Inventory
What materials are to be relocated, sold, scrapped, from the locations being consolidated, and what will be moved.

A location must be identified all that is retained; for product related raw material, work in process, finished goods; for supplies for production, warehousing, administration, maintenance; for shippable materials; sales and marketing literature.

Do some components feed more than one process? Recognize that fact in the layout.

7. Administrative and support

A location must be identified all that is retained; for equipment, furniture, fixtures, workstations.

♦ ♦ ♦

D. Status of destination facility

1. Understand physical characteristics of facility and grounds, capacities and limitations: dimensions, shape, condition; floor, dock, elevators, heights, weight limits. Mark the location of incoming utility, communications and service capacities, discharges, environmental risks and permits required; capability for expansion.

2. Don't forget roads, access and weight limits, parking, grounds.

3. Determine whether an acceptable layout will fit into the facility, or if it will be advisable to modify the building. If so, modify or construct as needed..

♦ ♦ ♦

Section on Facility Relocation, Merger, and Consolidation

Another commercial facility, in addition to or instead of?

Should an organization consider another facility, in addition to or instead of? Characteristics of the organization, the economy and of the facility marketplace will affect the answer. If a company opens a new facility, there will be costs and there may be benefits.

The single most important consideration is the most obvious, what does management want to do, where does management want to go? This decision may be subjective and / or consider objective criteria such as location of customers, suppliers, and technology; access to transportation, raw materials, and qualified workers.

The purpose of this book is to explore the factors, both objective and subjective, which affect the strategy, and suggest actions to optimize the benefits and reduce the costs.

Business strategy involves many elements, not the least of which is facility planning. Sales and costs share a common dependency on facilities, which must produce to meet sales demand at a low cost.

Some strategic objectives inherently influence the facilities plan; to expand or consolidate, acquire or divest or vertically integrate, make room for new products or utilize over capacity; all the while maintaining corporate image and satisfying management preferences. Many operating requirements for low costs are a function of the facility and its location, e.g. customer service; inventory levels; equipment capacity and utilization; labor, facility, and utility costs; qualified workers; technology; market and vendor access. The impact of these factors is apparent in the existing location or in other places, but costs and output can certainly be optimized in the existing facilities.

A company may consider a location for intangible reasons, such as management preference for a geographic area; management desire to reduce their living cost and tax load; sunshine, mountains, seashore, golf, tennis, skiing; less commuting time; to attract the increasing number of employees who prefer quality of life.

Fundamentals of facilities planning tend to remain constant, but objectives, economics, operating characteristics and preferences are unique to each company. Within the fundamentals, no two facility planning tasks are the same, because they are totally dependent on the client situations, strategy, and objectives.

Chapter 29   Overview, a facility instead of or in addition to

If your organization considers growth, merger, consolidation or relocation, through choice or because it has been imposed by market forces, there are many considerations for management to deal with other than facilities. But successful facility strategy is a major contributor to an effective, productive enterprise, because it optimizes the ways that operating entities work together to achieve the objectives of the organization.

A. Corporate strategy, and facility planning action to accomplish the strategy

The discussion below relates typical strategies and facility planning actions necessary, alone or in combination.

1. Improve operating utilization to optimize throughput and return on assets. Add new products, or adjust to a more profitable product mix.

> Quantify capacity of plant and support elements, constraints, loading, and utilization. Determine if the company should expand or relocate, or whether there are steps which would forestall a major facility change, e. g. relieve constraints; improve flow, cycle times, and inventory control.

2. Consolidate and merge facilities, equipment, and / or processes. Divest elements of the business

> Relocate products and equipment to be retained. Integrate production into the low cost configuration. Extricate useful equipment or facilities, and mothball, lease or liquidate the excess.

3. Acquire products, facilities, or equipment

> Evaluate the propensity of a facility or process to relocate or expand, and predict any potential problems, considering the equipment and process. Plan facilities for productivity and low cost at the required volumes. Add to, merge or relocate existing equipment or facilities.

4. Reorganize a division, plant, product line.

> Plan and implement rearrangement of facilities and equipment to gain efficiency from the reorganization.

5. Expand or relocate equipment or facilities for capacity purposes; reach new markets; cut operating or distribution costs; replace antiquated facilities; access technology, qualified workers, utilities; for quality of life or company image.

> Evaluate the propensity of a facility or process to relocate or expand, and predict any potential problems, considering the equipment and process. Plan facilities for productivity and low cost at the required volumes. Add to or relocate existing equipment or facilities

6. Search for another location to satisfy operating, cost, logistics, and subjective requirements of the corporation.

> To augment any of the actions above, find the most suitable site available. Compare expected location-sensitive costs in various communities, including one-time expense and capital as well as operational expense. Anticipate the magnitude of incentives, taxes, and tax abatements in different locations; negotiate with governments to optimize the advantage to the company.

◆ ◆ ◆

B.   Facility planning strategy and actions: not a moonshot

Nevertheless, some fundamental concepts, and proven actions, can ease a project, and increase the probability of success. That's what this book is about.

The organization should act very objectively, to determine the real facts and take serious steps to identify and quantify options. In the choice of what to do and where to do it, there are an immense number of possibilities. This book can help with the strategy and with actions, for you to apply to the circumstances, objectives, and preferences of your organization.

◆ ◆ ◆

C. Characteristics of a company who can consider another facility

Companies with several of the following characteristics may find that another facility offers attractive benefits:

1. Adequate size to make such an investment practical
      a. Sales of at least $50 to $100 million annually.

b. A potential to expand by some 100 or more jobs.

2. Company strategy would be reinforced by another facility
    a. The company has a desire to integrate vertically by extending the process upstream or downstream, or to have inventories located near the market.
    b. Additional qualified labor resources are needed and are scarce at the current location.
    c. The company practices manufacturing strategies of Just in Time, or continuous flow manufacturing, small lot sizes; which can be integrated with suppliers in another location.
    d. Conditions at a current facility are unsuitable, for any reason.
    e. Other facilities can be consolidated at one location to create economies of scale.

3. Major costs can be avoided at the existing facility by adding a facility elsewhere
    a. More manufacturing capacity is needed, and space to do so is limited or costly.
    b. Significant upgrade of facility is needed.
    c. Utilities are scarce or expensive.

4. Logistics would be improved
    a. Access to raw materials or components
    b. Shipping costs of finished products
    c. Customer service timing or access
    d. Velocity of transportation cycle

5. Environmental problems related to manufacturing are not serious
    a. Emissions and discharges from the process are not toxic, or if they are, equipment to reclaim, recycle, or treat is readily available.
    b. Water usage is not excessive.

6. The process is able to be recreated in another location
    a. The process may be technical and complex, but not overwhelmingly so.
    b. The process is in control and well documented now.
    c. Synergies would be created with another facility of the company's, a vendor, or a customer.

◆ ◆ ◆

D. A foreign company could find that a North American facility is attractive; if these characteristics apply as well as those in C.

The company sells in North America, or the product is especially designed for the North American market, or technology is based in North America.

    a. High duties into North America exist, or import quotas.

    b. Customer service requires rapid reaction from design or manufacturing, frequent model changes, product or people near the market, or rapid delivery of product or service into North America.

    c. New products are introduced frequently.

    d. Foreign exchange exposure can be minimized by manufacturing and selling in the same currency.

    e. Shipping causes inventory exposure, product damage or obsolescence.

    f. Upstream or downstream steps in the process already occur in North America.

Foreign owners who create jobs in the U. S. can qualify for a U. S. green card by investing a million dollars and creating twenty or so jobs. The investment can usually be reduced by half if the enterprise will be located in a rural area, or an urban area with an unemployment rate 150% of the national average. Incentives and / or tax breaks are often greater in these areas of high unemployment or economic need as well, in essentially all states.

♦ ♦ ♦

Chapter 30   Time to expand?? Time to relocate??

When is the time to expand, or to relocate? The following considerations are useful to determine which step, and when.

A. Time to expand ? ? ?

1. Favoring Expansion
   a. Facilities are crowded with people and equipment, and utilization is high.
   b. Vertical integration is favored, but no space is available.
   c. Sales are increasing.
   d. Overtime is prevalent.
   e. Inventories should increase. Back shifts are populated.
   f. Space is needed for new products, or new processes.
   g. Appropriate labor is scarce, or expensive

2. Suggesting no expansion, perhaps consolidation
   a. Facilities, people, and equipment are idle.
   b. More parts are being bought outside.
   c. Sales are decreasing.
   d. Overtime is rare.
   e. Inventories should decrease. Back shifts are not used.
   f. No space is needed for new products, or new processes.
   g. Labor is plentiful and well-priced.

3, Actions to avoid or delay expansion
   a. More throughput from people, equipment.
   b. Let vendors carry more of the load.
   c. Add overtime to bottleneck equipment.
   d. Rent outside space temporarily.
   e. Let vendors and customers carry inventory at their locations; increase turnover; practice JIT; convert previous storage space to productive space.

◆ ◆ ◆

B. Time to relocate ? ? ?

1. Favoring relocation
    a. Major customers are elsewhere, and shipping and / or customer service costs are significant.
    b. Location - sensitive costs are lower elsewhere: Labor rates, taxes, transportation in or out, energy, disposal of byproducts.
    c. There is a need to expand capacity, but a cost benefit to expand elsewhere.
    d. There is a need for a major rehabilitation of facilities, especially if existing facilities must produce continually.
    e. There is a need to escape political, labor, or organizational associations.
    f. Appropriate labor, utilities, technology, and / or outside support are scarce.
    g. Major suppliers are concentrated elsewhere and shipping costs are significant.
    h. Relocation incentives from other geographic areas are significant.
    i. Raw materials are available from widespread sources.
    j. Consolidation, integration, or product mix dictate a realignment of equipment or facilities, whether internal to the company, or with a vendor or customer.

2. Suggesting no relocation
    a. High cost to relocate people and / or equipment and processes.
    b. A strong geographical attraction to local customers or suppliers.
    c. There is a need to expand, but no cost benefit to expand elsewhere.
    d. Major investment in facilities difficult to move, with years of life remaining.
    e. Strong, favorable, political, labor, organizational, associations.
    f. Unique requirements for qualified labor

3. Actions to avoid or delay relocation
    a. Expand in place.
    b. Seek local concessions, grants, subsidies.
    c. Renegotiate contracts.
    d. More throughput from people, equipment.
    e. Let vendors carry more of the load.
    f. Add overtime to bottleneck equipment.
    g. Rent outside space temporarily.
    h. Let vendors and customers carry inventory at their locations; increase turnover; practice JIT; convert previous storage space to productive space.

♦ ♦ ♦

Chapter 31   Justification, both objective and subjective

The single most important consideration is the most obvious, what does management want to do, where does management want to go? This decision may be subjective and / or consider objective criteria such as location of customers, suppliers, and technology; access to transportation, raw materials, and qualified workers.

This chapter points out some of the objective and subjective factors to consider; both relocation incentives and quality of life will rate independent chapters later.

In a relocation, consolidation or expansion, there **WILL** be short term costs. There **MAY** be long term benefits. The purpose of justification is to anticipate the net effect of the strategy on a business. Both source and destination locations must be considered, as well as all ramifications, throughout the entire organization.

There are several location-sensitive costs, such as transportation, labor, utilities, taxes. A preliminary analysis can quantify these costs and create a short list of communities that meet management preferences as well as offer satisfactory costs. At this point organizations in the individual short-list communities can help identify the one best location. For instance, qualified economic development offices will list available property and potential incentives, and later provide a "one stop shopping" service for the permits and approvals necessary.

A. Action plan for project justification

Identify, quantify and compare one-time expenditures as well as operating costs and benefits at the current and at alternative new locations.

1. Compare the operating costs in the present location to forecasted operating costs in the proposed location, or location alternatives.
     a. Identify the costs which will vary by location.
     b. Learn enough about alternative locations to forecast variable costs there.
     c. Quantify the variable costs at the present location.
     Note: In this phase, the corporate financial, tax, cost accounting and general accounting professionals all have a significant role.

2. Compare the capital and one-time expense costs to acquire comparable facilities at the present location and at location alternatives.
     a. Estimate capital and one-time expense costs, if any, to upgrade the present facility to acceptable standards, of a size adequate for future capacity.

b. Estimate capital and one-time expense costs to acquire a facility in alternative locations to comparable standards, of a size adequate for future capacity.

c. Estimate capital and one-time expense costs to relocate the processes in question, and start them up again.

d. Estimate the costs to close or reduce operations at the current location, if this action is to be undertaken.

3. Compare the benefits available at the present and alternative locations.

a. Forecast the possible availability of grants, loans, and incentives to offset capital or expense spending for facilities. Investigate both local and at alternative locations.

b. Determine the possible availability of grants, loans, and incentives to offset capital or expense spending for operation. Investigate both local and alternative locations.

4. Consider any costs to operate multiple facilities

a. Transportation between, and travel to other facilities

b. Data communication lines, telephone, IT

c. Distribution, transportation of product to point of sale from multiple facilities

◆ ◆ ◆

B. Prices in the chosen destination community may minimize facility capital and operating cost

High cost element	Seek out in the destination city
Facility construction cost	Low construction cost area, in "down" cycle
	Land or financing provided by community
Labor cost	Low labor cost state
	Training provided by community
	Right to work state
High employee turnover	High unemployment
	Training provided by community
Material cost	Skilled labor pool
	Low employee turnover
Management cost	High quality of life
	Low personal taxes

Low cost of living
High unemployment

Waste and effluent cost	Area not already saturated, regulations are satisfactory
Water cost	Water is available, planning for future is sound
Energy cost is significant	Low energy cost, possibility of green energy on the property

♦ ♦ ♦

C. Green facility planning

"Green" facility planning is becoming a more significant factor in facility design, construction, maintenance and operation.

Such planning addresses the entire building lifecycle. The concept combines the benefit to the planet, with specific economic realities. Variation In local economics and priorities create many different payback calculation possibilities.

Primary factors usually include:
   Lower operating costs increase asset value
   Conservation of energy, water and other resources
   Occupant health and safety
   Money-saving construction incentives, tax rebates and zoning allowances

One organization which is deeply involved in green facility planning is Leadership in Energy and Environmental Design, or LEED. At its core, LEED is a program that provides third-party verification of green buildings. Major categories of the ratings criteria are: Sustainable Sites, Water Efficiency, Energy and Atmosphere, Materials and Resources, Indoor Environmental Quality. See http://www.usgbc.org/leed

Developed by the U.S. Green Building Council (USGBC), LEED is intended to provide building owners and operators a concise framework for identifying and implementing practical and measurable green building design, construction, operations and maintenance solutions, in an open and transparent process.

♦ ♦ ♦

Chapter 32   The marketplace which solicits business to locate in their areas

A. The marketplace

Businesses who seek another location will find an active marketplace composed of organizations whose objective is to attract new industry and business to their area.

The marketplace includes not only nations, states and communities, but utility and energy companies, railroads, air and water ports, geographic areas, financial organizations, enterprise zones, real estate companies and developers, industrial parks, research centers, educational institutions.

Businesses who consider a new site usually have different objectives from the communities where they search. A community will attract investment to itself regardless of its ability to meet the particular newcomer's requirements, while a company or organization seeks the one community which best satisfies their unique strategic objectives.

An effective way for a company to conduct a search is retain a consultant to establish its objective and subjective criteria, then sort through competing community claims. The consultant will confidentially and objectively evaluate the characteristics of several candidate locations compared to client standards. The client will not be identified until he is ready to take a public position. Even after a decision is made, confidentiality is vital because a company retains the best leverage over incentives and real estate costs before its identity is announced.

Industrial Development groups, politicians, realtors, financial institutions, technical or educational institutions are very helpful in the relocation process as they provide information, but early on a company should remain unidentified and be prepared to evaluate several locations carefully against its own criteria.

◆ ◆ ◆

B. A plan to identify a new location

The single most important consideration is the most obvious, where does management want to go? This decision may be subjective and / or consider objective criteria such as location of customers, suppliers, and technology; access to transportation, raw materials, and qualified workers.

There are several location-sensitive costs, such transportation, labor, utilities, taxes. A preliminary analysis can quantify these costs and create a short list of communities that meet management preferences as well as offer satisfactory costs. At this point organizations in the individual short-list communities can help identify the one best location. For instance, qualified economic development offices will list available property and potential incentives, and later provide a "one stop shopping" service for the permits and approvals necessary.

◆ ◆ ◆

C. Right to work

Twenty one states are "Right to Work" states, and under law stipulate that workers are not required to join a union in order to work in that state. Conversely, in all other states a union contract may require each worker to join the union as a condition of employment.

◆ ◆ ◆

D. Environmental concerns

Regulation of discharges, effluents, and waste disposal for environmental protection is increasing in all communities in the U. S. A., Canada, and Mexico. The controls will be a permanent feature in the future. Even with the controls, some communities are more rigorous because of existing conditions. Industrial companies will be more welcome in a community if they are aware of the local guidelines and intend to follow them in good faith. Even if the guidelines are rigorous, the resulting quality of life will allow industry to attract qualified people more readily, which in a high employment economy is a valuable asset.

For existing buildings, and on land to be purchased or disposed, at source or destination, give careful consideration to conditions that may require remediation, such as hazardous residue in the ground; lead or asbestos in the buildings; chemical, plating or painting facilities. These may not be a Super Fund site, or even a "showstopper" but they may be costly, require permits, extend the calendar. A formal Phase I, II, or III EPA inspection may be required before the property changes hands; put some time in the calendar.

◆ ◆ ◆

E. Owned or leased property; build or buy a facility

Many existing facilities are available for lease in communities. A company can minimize investment by leasing property until such time that investment is justified. Balance the benefit against the second move that would be required.

Whether leased or purchased, an existing facility may be made ready for use quickly, if the manufacturing process does not have special requirements or require major construction such as under-floor piping.

If construction is required, certain communities have a "sense of urgency" and rapid regulatory approval and construction is possible; in others the process takes longer.

◆ ◆ ◆

F. Permanent employees, or temporaries

Temporary employees are commonly utilized, by established organizations as well as by relocating ones. These employees can smooth out peaks and valleys in production, as well as limit permanent investment until the strategy of the business is clear and the market is established. Training of temporary as well as permanent employees will be funded by most states.

◆ ◆ ◆

Chapter 33   Relocation incentives and taxes

A. Once upon a time...

Communities offered big bucks to companies who would commit to bring jobs to the area.

Who	Where	When	Jobs	Incentive Reported million	/Job
Toyota	Georgetown Ky.	1986	3,000	$214	$71,333
BMW	Greer S. C.	1992	1,900	$155	$81,579
Mercedes	Vance Ala.	1994	1,500	$289	$192,667
Honda	Lincoln Ala.	1999	1,500	$165	$110,000
Nissan	Canton Miss.	2000	4,000	$299	$74,750
Toyota	Huntsville Ala.	2001	350	$29	$82,857
Hyundai	Montgomery Al	2002	2,000	$118	$59,000
Daimler Chrysler	Pooler Ga.	2002	3,200	$320	$100,000

(Later put on hold by company, before it broke up)

And then such incentives died down with the recession.

Will such incentives occur again?   The logic is still there from the community standpoint, that their investment will pay off over the years as taxes will be received from employment and the increased prosperity of the area. I am familiar with some of these towns, and the benefits from employment are obvious even when, or perhaps especially when, towns down the road are not doing so well.

However, even at the height of the headline deals, smaller incentives were much more common; numerous smaller towns have attracted businesses without a major incentive.

Federal, state and local authorities are in a perpetual dilemma, balancing budget pressures and the desire to attract new jobs. They typically provide incentives, then of course they tax the businesses they invited to the state. This chapter will summarize the types of

134

incentives and business taxes often found. Only a careful evaluation will define precisely the incentives and business taxes which will actually apply in a community, but good examples at least of the way it used to be, are explained below.

♦ ♦ ♦

B. State business and development incentives

The laws and regulations are established in many states to allow incentives to business, and bureaucracies are set up to encourage businesses and consider applications. Obviously, there is no guarantee of success when an application is made for assistance, but there is little cost to find out.

Some programs are readily funded by states and communities, for instance training assistance. Other programs, e. g. outright grants, are more difficult to obtain. Tax relief is common. Major concessions tend to involve facilities which generate many jobs, such as a new auto plant. Some companies are able to negotiate incentives, even though no formal program may be in effect.

Very few companies will have to finance their own infrastructure. Most communities provide water, sewer, utilities and power, access roads, and communications to industrial sites if they are not already in place. A business which requires access to seaports, airports, or railroads can find many sites where these are available.

Types of state programs are listed below. Not all states participate, and laws change quickly; only an inquiry and subsequent negotiation will generate a final package for the project.

1. Financing through Bonds; Industrial Development Bonds, State or Local Issue, Taxable Development Bonds, State or Local Issue

2. Grants; Incubator, Biotechnology, Industrial building renovation

3. Loans; Industrial Building Renovation, Jobs created

4. Financing; Innovation research, Tax increment financing for redevelopment, Private Development Credit Corporations

5. Training; pre-employment, on the job

6. Loan Guarantees; Based on jobs created. Rural Development, Export, Product commercialization

7. Tax Exemptions Possible, Principally to offset State Corporate Taxes; Job Creation Credit Per Job, Business Inventory, In-Transit, Freeport, Foreign Trade Zone, Pollution Control, Industrial Machinery, Industrial Fuels, Energy, Fuel Conservation, Enterprise Zone, Infrastructure credit, Corporate headquarters, Foreign trade Incentive, Property tax abatement, Minority subcontracts on state work

8. Some states, Texas and Georgia come to mind, provide help to companies who would expand locally; as a consultant I have lost relocation jobs to state subsidized professionals.

♦ ♦ ♦

C. Incentives from other members of the marketplace

Other organizations whose interests are served by attracting new industry and business may offer incentives as well as states. Counties, communities, utility and energy companies, railroads, air and water ports, geographic areas, financial organizations, enterprise zones, real estate companies and developers, industrial parks, research centers, educational institutions may well participate.

In some parts of the US, there is a surplus of available property; closed military bases and vacant textile plants are good examples. There may well be costs such as retrofit and perhaps hazardous substance residue, but the net cost of such a facility can be quite competitive.

To identify and quantify possible benefits from a variety of site options can be quite a job, and most companies do not have staff or experience to dig out the information. My suggestion is not self-serving; retain a consultant to help. A consultant can also maintain confidentiality as he investigates, and let me assure you,

A company has the most leverage with costs and incentives before it identifies itself.

♦ ♦ ♦

Chapter 34   Just where, exactly

If a project justification has been performed, and the indicated answer is to seek another location, then what? This chapter explains how to start the process to identify prime candidates.

The justification may well have indicated one or more locations which are favored for objective or subjective reasons.

A. The closed door discussions, concept phase.

Let me repeat, from an earlier chapter: "The single most important consideration is the most obvious, what does management want to do, where does management want to go? This decision may be subjective and / or consider objective criteria such as location of customers, suppliers, and technology; access to transportation, raw materials, and qualified workers."

The list of possible reasons is immense; so is the list of possible destinations. My professional belief is that for one organization in one set of circumstances there is one best location. Seattle or Sarasota? Bangor or Bakersfield? Compare and see. Remember, the best community for one organization will not necessarily suit another.

The executive who is first to consider consolidation or expansion or another location will make a few notes, then call someone else in, and close the door. Good thinking. Such strategic sessions will be full of "what if" scenarios, not ready for prime time. Keep them confidential.

♦ ♦ ♦

B. Still closed door, but a few more people in the room

Your organization may not be experienced in strategic concepts, either in the statement of justifications, definition of factors to be considered, or with the frameworks necessary to support investigation and implementation. Keep it quiet, but talk to all the players even, or maybe especially, those who might express valid questions or concerns about concepts and details.

Set up a process to assure an objective analysis. There will be ample opportunity for judgment, but to the extent possible let the data drive the decision.

Establish the requirements of the organization, so that potential actions, and later locations, may be measured against a common yardstick for both objective and subjective factors. Rank what is important to your organization; there is no right or wrong answer, just what fits the organization management style and priorities.

For instance, evaluate factors such as these:

1. Support required from a community
A company may require a wide variety of support functions, trained and semi-skilled people, professional services and vendors, communications and transportation infrastructure, utilities, and available property. The local community will commonly be expected to provide much of the support and people.

2. Operating cost
Significant portions of operating costs vary by location:
Labor cost according to skills, at all levels of the organization chart. Availability of temporary employees. Transportation of purchases to facility. Distribution, transportation of product to point of sale. Facility operating costs; utilities, energy, purchased services, waste disposal. Regulation by state and community. Taxes and offsetting incentives, see chapter 67.

3. Facility acquisition cost
A location with available low cost sites and buildings, or in which construction costs are low, is favored. The company may desire to lease facilities. In a down economy, real estate costs and availability tend to favor the one who can utilize the facility profitably.

4. Distance to customers, vendors, and technology
Other factors than cost contribute to successful operations; proximity to vendors can aid Just in Time sourcing; nearby customers can receive better customer service; sister plants in the organization may be in the same area.

When major auto companies open a new facility many of their suppliers will start operations nearby. This has been especially true of the southern cities mentioned in chapter 67, Incentives.

The presence of allied technology in an area can improve access to trained people and qualified support. Silicon Valley is the primary example of beneficial concentration within an industry, but many other communities and areas have existed or developed, often with community backing, to host allied companies.

5. Intangibles

Quality of life is a totally legitimate reason for choosing a facility location, and not only for executives. The people who work in the facility can choose to join you because of quality of life. Remember that QOL is in the eye of the beholder, one size does not fit all.

Corporate image can also be affected positively or negatively by location and by outward appearances of a facility.

♦ ♦ ♦

C. A project

Eventually a favored facility strategy will progress to a point where executives alone may not be able simultaneously to perform the tasks necessary, and run the business.

This is not just a blatant commercial, but consultants such as my company can often be quite useful in the first phases of a consolidation, expansion, relocation, another building instead of or in addition to. We bring four major benefits with us.

1. Objectivity, to evaluate and prioritize
2. Ability to dedicate time; we don't have an operation to run.
3. Another set of eyes, often experienced eyes.
4. Ability to investigate more confidentially, see chapter 71.

♦ ♦ ♦

Chapter 35   Site search process

To find a location community to meet managements objectives, undertake a site search. This chapter address ways to find a site.

A. A classic plan of action

The starting point is the list of operating requirements of the organization. This list is so that potential actions, and later locations, may be measured against a common yardstick for both objective and subjective factors. Rank what is important to your organization; there is no right or wrong answer, just what fits the organization management style and priorities.

From the list, develop a "long" list of candidate locations, perhaps even states. Choose the most desirable candidates; the "short" list.

From the short list, investigate and narrow down to the best candidate, the town and the specific property, all things considered. That's the destination.

◆ ◆ ◆

B. Other ways to find a suitable site

The long list of candidate communities can be crafted from careful criteria, or it may be set by a small group around a conference, or lunch, table. I've seen both ways.

It is not uncommon for a summary judgment to be handed down, "Why obviously we'll put it at the existing plant such and such, for economies of scale." That has happened, after a long and tedious search which did not include the plant early on.

I have outlined, over the phone, the attributes of several communities and the decision maker selected three for the short list. He later was quite happy with the final choice, one of the three.

So what site search action is correct? The purpose of investigation is to gain more confidence that the decision is correct, that as little money as possible is left on the table, that no really serious problem exists. But other factors are a time scale, and a budget, and the information that management already has gathered.

I would always recommend that a client carefully defines a list of requirements of the organization, as in Chapter 69, so we have a stationary target to shoot at. Then whether a list has twelve or three or two is a minor matter.

Please note that a site search must be completed before a final project justification is calculated in order to assure an accurate expectation of the destination costs.

◆ ◆ ◆

C. The working tools to collect information

In this day of the Internet, finding really useful information about a community is very easy and user friendly. Check out http://www.yesvirginia.org, my favorite not only because of the name but also because they do such a good job when you arrive in Richmond; also check out http://www.ecodevdirectory.com/north_carolina.htm. Both these states are pros, and their track record shows it.

There are non-state sites for quality of life, for electric and gas prices, for cost of living, unemployment rates, trucking costs, on and on.

The state and community sites can assist, but remember their objective is to attract your organization to their location. That is not the same as your objective, to find the best location for your interests. And I reiterate, a company has the most leverage before it reveals its identity.

◆ ◆ ◆

D. Evaluate the long list

Usually the long list can be evaluated long distance, through the internet and over the telephone. Just mention to an industrial development person that you are interested, and get set for incoming mail and phone calls and e-mail for weeks, from them and realtors, utilities, services. This in itself is reason enough to use a consultant; to avoid the attention. They usually just send us what we ask for, so we aren't so inundated.

Compare what you find out to the requirements list. Be prepared to adjust the requirements; you will find that something is available that you hadn't considered. Maybe you will be led to other cities.

At this point it will be necessary to start to evaluate and compare what you learn. Is the wage rate more or less important than electricity, than the proximity of a big airport, than the availability of a local machine shop? There is no formula for such relationships; it will depend entirely on your particular needs.

Perform analysis to evaluate what you learn and create a short list of communities that meet management preferences as well as offer satisfactory costs.

◆ ◆ ◆

E. Evaluate the short list

Start out this phase by long distance also, but be prepared to travel, and to deal with industrial development people and realtors face to face. Remember, the client has the strongest bargaining position for costs and incentives before he reveals his identity.

Organizations in the individual short-list communities can provide very useful information from long distance. For instance, qualified economic development offices will cover all economic and cost factors, and also list available property for view, often in great detail. Local and national commercial realtors will do the same. States and communities will preview potential incentives, although a final agreement will require serious commitment and negotiations.

The site search is not over until the actual property is identified and acquired, leased, or bought. A community may be a fine choice, but unless there is a satisfactory property there, it's all academic.

Be prepared to modify ideas, adapt, think outside the box. A candidate town or property may be perfect, except... If you can find a way to accommodate the flaw in a way that doesn't sacrifice a true value, the choice may still be superior to others.

Be sure to look for communities which provide a "one stop shopping" service for the permits and approvals necessary, because approvals are likely to take a long time at best.

◆ ◆ ◆

Chapter 36   Quality Of Life, and Culture Shock

Quality of Life can be a deciding factor in site selection, so don't overlook its importance. Different features appeal to different individuals, but management preferences are always important. Is it valid to choose a site because it is a nice place to live? Absolutely.

There are many instances of culture shock; often of people overseas, but also in people who find themselves in a new part of their own country. This intangible subject is perhaps different to everyone who considers it. Because of that difference, Quality of Life should be carefully considered by the company, selecting and evaluating those factors considered to be important. Management may want to live in the area where the facility is, but even if it doesn't, quality of life is increasingly important to those who will work in the facility. A favorable life style will attract qualified people to the location.

Some quality of life elements can be quantified, such as cost of living, schools, medical facilities, crime rates, taxes. Others are more subjective; do you like to walk the beach or ski? Do you like the features of a big city or the quiet of a small town?

Web sites identify communities considered to be good places to live.

The following list is designed to enumerate Quality of Life elements, but QOL is in the eye of the beholder and the list may not be adequate for all. Fill it out for the community being considered, and the results will start to characterize the community. Then, decide if that community is right for you and your company. Search the web for specific information, e. g. commuting time.

Location

Ranking in national survey:
        survey: date:

Amusements
        Amusement Parks

        Auditoriums, arenas

        Bowling Alleys

        Fairs, Festivals

        Movie Houses

        Newspapers

Night Clubs

Radio Stations: AM   FM

Television: Local Stations   Received   Cable Available

Climate
    Mean Summer temperature   Mean Winter temperature
    Annual days of sunshine   Annual rainfall

Colleges, Universities   Affiliation   Enrollment

Commuting, Travel
    Size of town
    Travel crosstown   Miles   Time
    Interstate, limited access highways
    Residential districts relationship to industrial locations

Cultural
    Concert Halls
    Dance company
    Music, Live
    Museums, Galleries
    Orchestra
    Theaters: Professional   Amateur

Dining out
    Restaurants: Local cuisine   International   Fast Food

Education
    Public Schools: elementary   middle   high
        Pupil / teacher ratio $ / pupil spent
        Accreditation

    Private Schools: elementary   middle   high
        Pupil / teacher ratio $ / pupil spent
        Accreditation
        Affiliation

Historical features
    Name   History

Medical
    Doctors   Dentists   Eye care
    Hospitals   Beds   Clinics   Nursing Homes

Natural attractions nearby
 Bodies of Water
 Name   .Powerboat, Fish, Beach, Swim. Sail

 Camping

 Canoe, kayak

 Hunting

 Mountains, hiking, mountain biking

 National Parks

 Parachute jumping

 Private aviation

 Skiing

 State Parks

Newspapers available
 Local   Area   National

Organizations
 Charitable Organizations
 Children's sports: Baseball   football   soccer   other
 Libraries
 Scouting: Boy Scouts   Girl Scouts
 Service or Fraternal Organizations
 Women's Organizations

Outdoor recreation
 Country Clubs

 Golf Courses, nine hole: public   private
         nine hole: public   private   ratings

 Public Parks   Swimming Pools   Forests   Lakes

 Trails: Hiking   Biking   Horse

 Tennis courts, indoor   outdoor   lighted

 Zoo

Professional sports
 Sport   .   Affiliation

145

Religious
      Churches Available

Shopping
      Malls   Total stores represented
      Stores: Clothing   Department   Drug
      Grocery   delicatessen   bakeries
      Books   electronics

Chapter 37   The need for confidentiality

In an expansion or relocation project, confidentiality is a constant concern. A company will develop and evaluate strategic options regarding facility placement, and these options will usually affect individuals, groups, and communities. It is mandatory that those considering the options do not accidentally divulge information prematurely because the potential for damage is great. Executives consider confidential options routinely but relocation or expansion require assistance from more levels within the company and of course from outside.

Please let me repeat.
A company has the most leverage with costs and incentives before it identifies itself.

A. Outside the company

There is a basic contradiction between site search and confidentiality; the first is information and the second is lack of information. The key is to balance these contradictions; learn of a community while shielding the company until it is ready to take a public position; after a decision has been made and not before.

It will be necessary to establish mechanisms to maintain confidentiality inside and outside the company. Confidentiality does not require the services of an international spy, but sometime the physical arrangements give that impression. This statement is not self-serving, but a consultant can represent a company confidentially because the logistics are easier for him.

Let me tell you sometime the story of a corporate jet, visiting a potential site, which was misidentified as a drug smuggler; police met the plane and demanded identification. Vice presidents don't like Air Force fighters on the wing tips, nor the local sheriff and the FBI who met the plane and demanded identification.

A few years back, the manufacturing VP of a Cleveland company visited the Mayor of San Antonio while looking for a relocation site; within two days his visit and its subject were on the front page of the Plain Dealer, and every local politician from Cleveland and San Antonio was on the phone. It turned out that the Mayor's daily schedule was public information.

In this age of the internet there is more rapid access to information. Search for a telephone number, or an address and receive instant confirmation of a company. Check Linked In for a name and your executive is identified.

The moral of these horror stories of course is that it is difficult to maintain confidentiality until the company is ready to take a more visible position. But, and this is not just an advertisement, a consultant can represent a company confidentially because the logistics are easier for him. His name, address, company, phone, web site are all common knowledge.

In this electronic age, confidentiality is much more difficult to maintain for a company employee.

He or she must not leave a name or company or title or phone number or fax, nor use an email address if it is in the name of the company, or otherwise traceable. In this day of caller ID and user profiles, a company employee can give away an identity pretty easily. A slip-up can occur because of what ID is on the briefcase or stationery, what you record at the hotel and car rental counter.

When word gets out that a company is seeking a site, the marketplace will flood the company with attention. A confidential search by a consultant can shield a client from this flood, from political pressure, and from unwanted publicity, especially early in the process before basic decisions are made. A consultant can also determine real estate prices and incentives before the company is known, in order to maximize leverage early in the project. The consultant will evaluate the claims made by locations objectively, compared to the client standards. States, communities, and organizations will readily cooperate with a consultant representing an unnamed client, although not as positively as when they later welcome the CEO to their town.

Politicians make extravagant promises too; one mayor said she would furnish a recipe for chicken fried steak. Regretfully I couldn't collect when we chose another town.

♦ ♦ ♦

B. Within the company

Until announcements are made by the client company, internal confidentiality is equally important. Older rules still apply but you will have to work at it. Limit information on a need-to-know basis; watch what you say, what you write and distribute, who you call, what credit cards you use, who sees expense accounts and credit card bills.

Inform those who will assist within the company; be sure that they know management's plan well so they can meet the objectives. There may well be several internal disciplines involved, to identify and evaluate options. But impress them with the need for

148

confidentiality, and provide the support they need to maintain it. Because you and the teams will be asking many questions in many places, establish a logical rationale for the questions.

Plan to make a public announcement as soon as possible. Just in case, name a contact with responsibility for publicity, media and the public. Sooner or later a news reporter or camera crew will show up, and it will be better to have your information and spokesperson prepared.

◆ ◆ ◆

Chapter 38   Red flags and warning signs

Warning signs can occur at any phase of a project. Following are some examples, both particular red flags and general categories.

A. For your current, source, location,

A "yes" response to these questions raises a red flag. Even expansion alone may be problematic.

a. Extensive waste treatment or environmental protection is required.
b. Management people would not welcome a relocation.
c. Critical technical people would not welcome relocation.
d. It would be difficult to accumulate inventory to last through a relocation.
e. There are unique requirements for qualified labor, which can be met in the current area.
f. Operating processes are poorly defined and written.
g. Unusual cleanup will be required of the vacated premises

♦ ♦ ♦

B. Environmental concerns

Regulation of discharges, effluents, and waste disposal for environmental protection is increasing in all communities in the U. S. A., Canada, and Mexico. The controls will be a permanent feature in the future. Even with the controls, some communities are more rigorous because of existing conditions. Industrial companies will be more welcome in a community if they are aware of the local guidelines and intend to follow them in good faith. Even if the guidelines are rigorous, the resulting quality of life will allow industry to attract qualified people more readily, which in a high employment economy is a valuable asset.

For existing buildings, and on land to be purchased or disposed, at source or destination, give careful consideration to conditions that may require remediation, such as hazardous residue in the ground; lead or asbestos in the buildings; chemical, plating or painting facilities. These may not be a Super Fund site, or even a "showstopper" but they may be costly, require permits, extend the calendar. A formal Phase I, II, or III EPA inspection may be required before the property changes hands; put some time in the calendar.

♦ ♦ ♦

C. Processes that can cause relocation issues

Heavily plumbed process, floor drains

High ceilings, such as for material handling overhead cranes

Weight requirements for floor mounted process equipment

Unusually wide equipment

Unusual boiler requirements

Process generated hazardous waste for disposal

Equipment mounted in pits, or heavy foundations

Is comfort air conditioning required? Process A/C?

Special air quality, temperature, pressure rooms

High requirements for power, water, gas, sewer

◆ ◆ ◆

D. At the destination

If chosen building requires significant modification beforehand; some actions might be scheduled after the move for instance add-ons for storage or office. A special case is that a choice might be fine except it has too few toilets for today's zoning, and sewage lines are undersized.

If chosen property requires a zoning change.

◆ ◆ ◆

E. Timing issues can arise if

Short time window is available, particularly if dates are fixed.

Operation can't be out of business readily

F. Logistics

Will current employees not move with the business, amplifying technology transfer issues?

Is there a floor layout of the existing facility? Of the new facility? An accurate inventory of equipment? Do not assume they are correct, at your peril.

You will face the question of insurance for the equipment that you relocate while it is the mover's responsibility. There is no one constant answer, yes you should insure or no, you needn't. Nor will you have a firm idea of the dollar limits of the policy. The cost will be higher than you think is necessary, and you will consider the possibility of a problem to be slight. But you must balance the cost and likelihood of loss against the size of the risk and the damage to your business if a moving van were to be in an accident, or a computer CPU dropped.

Moves are not business as usual, and otherwise rigid security rules may be relaxed unintentionally. Be sure to protect the confidential aspects and intellectual property of the business during a move, as well as the physical assets.

◆ ◆ ◆

G. What you see is what you get? Maybe not.

Many concerns may be out of sight in this day and age. The following are worth mentioning, but there will be others.

Lead, in old pipes or paint, may have to be removed.

Asbestos, as an insulation around pipes or in walls or ceilings, may have to be removed.

Drainage; see the property after a rainstorm. Understand how a problem can be corrected, considering the law and effect on neighbors.

Foundations; are they what they seem?

Termites, in wood buildings. In the same category, wood rot.

Soil; in at least two ways. If you will build now or later, you should have soil borings to determine the capacity to support a structure. And, even if you will not build, what is under the soil? Do you expect to grow something and the top soil is only a veneer over a gravel bed?

Environmental survey, phase I, II, III. An official survey performed by an authorized environmental consultant will determine the existence of serious problems, such as buried fuel tanks, toxic residue from previous processes, buried historical sites, Indian mounds, wetlands, old dumps.

Roof; its condition and your expectations. Modern testing methods can define condition better than before, but roofs have finite lives.

Determine the easements for the new property, written and unwritten. Easements usually concern utilities and access to the property, but in one instance a third party had been granted access to rest rooms; it was news to the incoming tenant.

Are there emissions from your operation that will affect the neighbors? Vice versa? In this modern day, don't forget electronic emissions. One client's RF heaters were a source of concern at a nearby airport.

◆ ◆ ◆

Chapter 39   Master Plan for a campus, of multiple facilities

A facility master plan layout is the arrangement of all of the components required for a business to perform its charter. It is the broad view of design, layout, and the arrangement of people, materials and machines.

Master planning may be tailored to a property, to a building, or to an entire campus, depending on an organization's objectives. Chapter 56 addresses master layout planning for a facility and this chapter addresses a campus type operation.

I have worked on business campuses, and had the opportunity to help create one as well. The normal facility guidelines apply, but there is also a need to think on a larger scale, in a longer time frame, than perhaps we are accustomed. This chapter will point out some considerations and ramifications for facility planning.

The key is to plan a facility that will be effective on day one and expandable into the final configuration that is anticipated.

The Block Layout Concept, as described in Chapter 47, is very useful in master planning. The block layout determines the overall dimensions of an group of activities or department and draws them as one piece, a "block" of floor space. A block layout is very useful to evaluate, and to differentiate, general arrangement options within a building. It will allow flow planning between groups or functions. It will also make sure that all pieces of the operation will fit into the chosen area in the first place.

Block layout provides a visual aid to compare how different arrangements would provide for production efficiencies, flow, space utilization, growth, access. A block layout before final selection can also point out necessary building or property improvements and modification.

♦ ♦ ♦

A. There will be a business plan or model and local communities involved
Understand what is promised and signed; business models and plans, probably covering phases over time. Agreements and contracts with communities and others. Facilities, operations, amenities to be provided in the campus. What buildings are there now, integration plan and options.

♦ ♦ ♦

B. Placement of the overall facility on the property

A prime objective is not to block future usage by initial placements.

Plenty of people will participate regard in their areas of expertise; consultants; architects and engineers, soil borers, contractors and subs, lawyers. The community will have requests or demands, as well as architectural standards and regulations to meet.

At least the following factors will be involved. None of them need be a critical problem, but there will be only one chance to plan the best fit, and that is at the beginning.

1. Access
Plan for roads, rail, and water access very early, and integrate into the overall plan to serve both short and long arrangements. Where are roads, rail, water, for incoming materials and outgoing product. Position the in and out docks, roads and traffic flow very early in a convenient location where they do not later interfere with expansion on the property.

2. The lay of the land
On the property, are there hills / valleys / water / low land that will be expensive to utilize? How can you avoid them without affecting operations? Can buildings be placed to avoid moving earth? Earth moving is expensive and usually does not add value.

Read the topographical maps, walk the property, locate and evaluate the layout impact of hills and wetlands; rocks and trees. Don't forget easements, overhead constraints, building offsets, curbside appeal, earthquake, wind, snow, local requirements such as flood plain.

3. Services to the property
Many services will be used on the campus, and it is best to consider early how and where to connect to feed mains.

Understand needs and regulations, then evaluate location options for power, heat, water, gas, telecom, wireless, sanitary sewage and storm drains, grey water, fire protection, rail access, water access, air access, curb cuts, green energy generators, communication structures. Fire tanks or lakes, fire water lines and hydrants. Security fence, gates, electronics.

4. Property Geometry
Does property require buildings be long and slender, square shaped, ells, etc.

C. Plan for growth, within a master plan

Objective: Don't block the future usage by initial placements. As well as the crystal ball permits, create a campus to use space effectively and provide efficient flow patterns for operations.

It is usually not a problem to build one facility for one product and later to add similar facilities for other products and / or volume. Try to anticipate growth and leave room in the master plan to do so.

The same is true for vertical integration; you may purchase parts initially, with a plan for a facility to make the component in-house in future years. Be sure to leave an empty location in the master plan.

Are other products anticipated but not identified, that you can provide for at this time? On the campus plan it is easy to specify a site even if it is not clear what is to occupy it in future years. Process flow may turn out to be inconvenient, but the master plan should provide avenues for materials handling and future technology, even if detail is lacking until later.

How will the campus deal with future rapid or technologically comprehensive changes? Try to allow space, even if the future requirements are not firm.

◆ ◆ ◆

Chapter 40   A "simple" move

A. Assumptions

Product is being manufactured at point A, the source.
Product is to be manufactured at point B, the destination.
It is not necessary to select point B, justify a move, select alternatives.
Technology is relatively straightforward and well documented at the source.

♦ ♦ ♦

B. Charter

There is little strategy involved; the charter is to find out what the process and product needs, provide it at the destination, and relocate on schedule (quickly) and on budget.

♦ ♦ ♦

C. Outline of steps in the relocation

Determine what is provided at the destination
Determine process requirements at the source
Identify and deal with Show Stoppers
Adapt the destination to meet requirements as necessary.
Prepare the process for relocation
Relocate physically. Install the process at the destination.

♦ ♦ ♦

D. Detail of steps in the relocation

These are typical necessary steps leading to the startup of a process at a destination. Some steps may be done by the client at the source or the destination, some may be assigned to a consultant. JPR is capable of performing any or all steps. Early in the project a comprehensive list will be made, specific assignments given and a timetable set.

1. Determine what is provided at the destination
   a. Facility: Space, utilities, waste disposal, environmental permits.
   b. Technical: Skills required of people in manufacturing, test, engineering, and quality. Availability of people to assign to the manufacturing and support groups as well.

c. Hardware, software, manual systems now in use for manufacturing and materials management, purchasing, inventory control, scheduling, cost accounting, finished goods warehouse and shipping.

2. Determine process requirements at the source
   a. Facility: Space, utilities, waste disposal, environmental permits.

   b. Technical and engineering
      1. Skills required and manning
      2. Bills of material. Routers. Component, subassembly, and product specs, current and historical. Labor, material, and cost standards. Direct labor crewing, indirect labor applied specifically to the product and to general support groups. Cycle times.
      3. Operator instructions. Test requirements and programs.
      4. Manufacturing and testing equipment, tools, gages, fixtures, material handling equipment, spare parts lists and inventories, maintenance histories, preventive maintenance and calibration schedules.
      5. Process layout and flow for manufacture and test. Space for support functions.

   c. Hardware, software, manual systems now in use for manufacturing and materials management, purchasing, inventory control, scheduling, cost accounting, documentation, finished goods warehouse and shipping. Component and supply item vendors, prices and outstanding commitments both ways, and purchasing files.

3. Show Stoppers
After review of source and destination circumstances, are there potential problems which could seriously delay the project? Some possibilities which could extend the critical path include:
   a. Insufficient inventory to allow the source to shut down.
   b. Long lead time construction necessary at the destination.
   c. Permitting necessary at the destination.
   d. Complex technology transfer including the people involved; and / or poor documentation at the source in key topics.
   e. Incompatible electronics, hardware, or software between source and destination.
   f. Overly optimistic learning curve assumed at the destination.

4. Adapt the destination to meet requirements as necessary.
      a. Space for manufacture, test, inventory and support activity.
      b. Make layouts of equipment and process flow, get approval. Mark the locations of all to be moved and services.
      c. Get permits, relocate existing equipment, run utilities, and waste disposal as needed.

5. Prepare the process for relocation

     a. Inventory equipment, supplies and inventories to be moved. List, code and mark it. Inventory equipment, supplies and inventories <u>not </u>to be moved. List, code, mark it.

     b. Videotape the existing operation for benchmark purposes.

     c. Collect paper and electronic specs, instructions, records, management systems for component and product manufacture, test and shipment; equipment maintenance; inventory and scheduling; finance; sales and marketing. Collect historical records of product development; of startup; of incoming component inspection; of customer purchases and warranties; of product brochures and sales literature.

     d. Find reliable riggers and movers. Get quotes. Award and schedule the move.

◆ ◆ ◆

E. Relocate physically.

     Install the process at the destination.
     Oversee the move at source and destination.
     Dispose of items not to be needed at the destination.

◆ ◆ ◆

Chapter 41   A "simple" expansion

 A web searcher asked recently about expansion, as business was good and his company needed a "simple" expansion, if there is such a thing. My reply follows. "Thanks for the inquiry. I'm glad to hear that sales are increasing, so that you can expand your operations.

There will be several factors to consider, such as the following, more or less in this sequence:

A. Space and building
Quantify the desired product capacity for output, starting at the finished product. Calculate what this output volume requires at each of the preceding, upstream stages in your process; also take advantage of the opportunity to think about any operations you might want to perform in-house instead of purchasing.

Review product mix and the effect on equipment requirements.

List pieces of equipment required to reach the sales capacity, at each step. This will include speeds, manning, hours worked.

Calculate the operating space required for equipment, raw material, in-process, finished goods.

Estimate the space required for support activity and personnel for an operation and headcount as defined in long term plans.

Determine the number of people required, and outline the plan to retain and train them.

Think about how future growth should be planned, now, so that you do not block future expansion in this phase.

The resulting space should approximate the building size, and additions necessary.

As for the existing property size, will it hold the larger building? Is there a possibility to use multi-level operations? Are changes to access, roads, utility feeds indicated? Will permits and approvals, and their timing, pose any calendar problems?

Evaluate and choose financing options.

Set overall timing, and project phases during the sequence of expansion. How will you phase the addition and the present operations? Will the operation continue without interruption, or will it have to phase into the expansion?

Is there new technology desired for process, equipment, controls?
      Continuous or batch processing
      Kind of equipment, possible upgrades.
      State of the art technology
      Material handling

ISO or other regulatory technology
      How do ISO norms differ from your current practice? There may be two main categories; the ability of equipment to perform to spec, and a process control system that you must develop and apply. Determine how the company intends to conform to ISO or other regulatory requirements, and build that into the plans.

◆ ◆ ◆

B. Layout

Determine which specific equipment is desired, for the technology, product mix, and capacity characteristics.

Integrate the flow through equipment and materials handling.

Layout the equipment within a building, either existing or new

◆ ◆ ◆

C. Implementation

Plan construction, buy equipment. Hire and train. Each of these will require a specific plan, to be developed when earlier questions are answered.

This outline covers many of the issues to be resolved. Other sections of this book will cover particular subjects more closely.

◆ ◆ ◆

Chapter 42   Create a facility from scratch

A. Summary

There are very many tasks to create a facility from scratch but they often fall into a relatively simple sequence:

1. Define a transition plan
2. Understand the existing process, quantify what is to be installed in the new facility
3. Compile documentation adequate to operate the process
4. Create a new facility which provides for the process
5. Provide acceptable materials, components, supplies at the destination
6. Obtain equipment for the new facility, and move it there
7. Place equipment, material, and documentation in the new facility
8. Hire and train people to operate the facility
9. Start up the facility

◆ ◆ ◆

B. Detail of actions in the relocation sequence

1. Define a transition plan
   a. Scope, timing, budget
   b. Materials: vendors for components at destination; inventory plans; learning curve; support from another facility
   c. Management, technical support from U. S. and from source country
   d. Commitments to buyers of finished goods
   e. Specific action assignments, critical path, timetable, and monitoring techniques.
   f. Are there state and local incentives and tax relief possible? Plan to claim them.

2. Understand the existing process, quantify what is to be installed in the new facility

Facility, process, direct and support equipment; tooling and fixtures; direct and indirect materials, commodities, and supplies; material handling and warehouse equipment; administration needs. Bills of material, routers. Equipment sizes and utility needs Layout and process flow. Raw material, work in process points and amounts, finished goods inventory levels and warehouse cube criteria.

3. Compile documentation adequate to operate the process

Equipment, spare parts, maintenance and preventive maintenance records, drawings, manuals, electronic files, Cad Cam, calibration, tools and gages. Bills of material, process flowcharts, routers; process detail, work instructions; labor hours standard and actual; capacity calculations, learning curve information; operator training plan and video of operations; acceptable reclaim processes. statistical quality plan and history; limit samples of components and product; quality history. Translate documents if necessary.

4. Create a new facility; new or modified, leased or owned.
   a. Block and detailed layouts for facility, production, support, and administration. Growth plan for expected new products.
   b. Plan building, determine the distribution of services, effluent, HVAC, telecommunications, environmental, fire and safety requirements. Obtain local approvals, permits, licenses. Qualify contractors, bid and let contracts, assure contractor compliance. Arrange security.
   c. Monitor progress relative to time line, see that contractor pays subs, administer construction accounting to protect client interests, verify quality level of construction, approve invoices for payment. Prepare punch list at completion, see that work is finished, approve final payments.
   d. Set up accounts for utilities, and for those groundskeeping, maintenance, housekeeping and security functions that will be outsourced.

5. Provide acceptable materials, components, supplies at the destination.
   a. Define what is required: Specifications, for components and product involved; packaging and artwork; inspection criteria. Material and supply bills, usage standard and history, Master Standard Data Sheets for chemicals, approved supplier list, vendor records, master production schedule techniques.
   b. Set up vendor lists for all materials, in the destination or other countries.
   c. For vendors in the destination countries, translate spec, establish quality levels and acceptance procedures, packaging, delivery, prices, payment terms, lead times, inventory plans. Get trial product.
   d. For vendors in other countries, arrange shipments, timing, transportation, customs and duty procedures, security, inventory plans.
   e. Establish a materials flow plan, Just in Time or Just in case. Set objectives for inventory of raw material, WIP, finished goods. Make a contingency plan for alternate sources of supply.

6. Hire and train people to operate the facility
Decide whether to have permanent or temporary employees. Select local agencies.

Locate and train qualified operators, technical and support people, supervision. Set up trainers and programs for those who will be sent to the source for training and for those who will receive vestibule and job training on site. Determine when people should be hired and trained in order to meet production plans. Establish manning plan, learning curve and expectations by job.

7. Obtain equipment and materials for the destination facility, and move it there, both new and relocated.
   a.   At the source location, tag, pack, rig, ship equipment and materials being transferred. Arrange customs, duty, and shipping.
   b.   Write specs for equipment and materials being purchased, obtain and let bids. Arrange for vendor shipment, customs, duty.

8. Place equipment, material, and documentation in the new facility
At the destination, unpack transferred and new equipment, locate, install, hook up services and utilities. Use documentation package to assure that transferred and new equipment is properly installed. Run qualification tests for new equipment to assure that specs have been met.

9. Start up the facility
Place trained operators at qualified equipment, with appropriate documentation and approved materials. Start operations. Increase output according to predetermined learning curve expectations.

◆ ◆ ◆

Chapter 43   Consolidation, merger, of equipment, facility or process

My friend Michael Gendron has practiced M & A for years, has written books such as "Creating the New E-Business Company", "Integrating Newly Merged Organizations", "Doing the M & A Deal: A Quick Access Field Manual & Guide", "A Practical Approach to International Operations". Mike heads CFO Insight at http://www.cfoinsight.net.

I will leave the broader M & A detail to Michael, but my objective here is to address an important portion of M & A, where an organization's strategy is to <u>consolidate processes, facilities and equipment,</u> previously belonging to more than one organization or entity. An organization will want to create an integrated, effective, productive enterprise which maximizes operating and distribution synergies from the previous individual elements.

A physical consolidation can be successfully created. The purpose of this chapter is to identify issues which can apply, and not only layout, so that the organization can assign them comprehensively to internal and external resources in different disciplines and locations. To resolve many of these issues, it will take more than an M & A consultant.

Issues are arranged in these categories:

A. Background
B. HR Issues
C. Integrate operations of companies involved
D. Integrate electronic and manual systems of companies involved
E. Inventory plan during transition
F. Customer relationships
G. Vendor relationships
H. Day to day operation
I. Status of existing facility
J. Plan for relocation: process and technology, equipment, inventory, support and administrative.
K. Prepare the destination facility
L. Complete the relocation itself
M. Start up the relocated equipment with the trained operators

In each section, several questions must be addressed. More or less in sequence, they are: What elements at the source will remain the same and what will be changed during the transition; what internal and external resources are assigned to the topic from among the original organizations; what is the precedence of events and the timetable for completion.

Each resource may be assigned several tasks, and the individual priority and responsibility within the entire scope must be clear for successful completion.

♦ ♦ ♦

A. Background

Define carefully, strategy and objectives, timetable, budget and scope of the project.

1. Responsibility of each entity involved, and what they must deliver as their part of the scope and when it is required; especially process, technology, facilities, equipment, and cooperation during the transition.

2. Internal resources of each organization involved who will be assigned to the project.

3. Communication to participants.

♦ ♦ ♦

B. H. R. Issues

A merger by nature is likely to involve personnel actions. Address what H. R. actions will be taken to accomplish the financial objectives of the merger, what company policy is regarding the actions, and timetable for announcements and actions.

1. Define the destination organization chart and approximate numbers of people.

2. Compare to existing organization charts at source plants and define potential changes.

3. Explore the comparative aspects of personnel transfer to early retirement or termination and rehire, considering company policy. Set a plan to be followed.

4. Project the likely action to attain the desired destination organization, person by person in the management and administration structure; who will be retained, transferred, retired, let go.

5. Project the likely action to attain the desired destination organization for key employees just below the management level, person by person.

6. Project hourly employee totals; how many will be retained, transferred, retired, let go. Define pay and expense policy for hourly people who travel as trainers.

7. Project an attrition rate of those who will be asked to transfer and will decline, and the secondary plan to fill those jobs. Identify key participants and what-if scenarios if they leave during the project.

8. Plan the announcement process and timing. (My own experience: full and complete, as soon as possible. Logistically, it is hard to contain news of a consolidation project of any size, and a formal announcement is much more professional than a reaction when a rumor starts as it inevitably will A first announcement may be made without specific names, but with general guidelines that the company will utilize.)

9. Set up mechanisms, and people to administer them, to deal with termination, retirement, transfer, and new hire.

10. Name a person to speak for the company to the media. Relocations are usually big time news locally.

♦ ♦ ♦

C. Integrate operations of companies involved

1. Determine all production equipment; which will be most useful to meet output, quality, product mix and cost objectives in the final configuration.

2. Consider any new process technology to add during the consolidation.

3. Consider any new management control or planning system to be implemented during the consolidation.

4. List any required upgrades, modifications or maintenance during the consolidation.

5. Plan to idle and keep any equipment which could become useful as future volume or product mix changes.

6. In case of a regulated product whose manufacturing location must be certified, the timing will be extended.

♦ ♦ ♦

D. Integrate electronic and manual systems

1. Keep or change identification numbers of similar / identical products?

2. Inventory control, allocation system and changes planned as equipment is relocated. Software to be installed on hardware at the destination? Raw material, WIP, finished goods.

3. Keep or change the system for physical coding of inventory location?

4. Accounting, financial systems integration / independence. One or more cost centers from financial standpoint. New overhead allocation? Please don't transfer it as-is.

5. Customer base management integration / independence.

◆ ◆ ◆

E. Inventory plan during transition

1. Bill of material components, by SKU. Date vendors will change place of delivery.

2. Discontinuation of SKU's or commodities.

3. Supply acquisition and recordkeeping.

4. Buildup of finished goods to cover production interruption.

5. Parallel operation of shipping or shutdown during transition; dates.

6. Integration of new stock into existing stock; physical location and / or systems.

◆ ◆ ◆

F. Customer relationships

1. Advise customers of new address, phone, fax; change in account rep or contact. Advise in any changes of procedure or paperwork, shipping company, timing, billing, terms, etc.

2. Work out advanced, delayed, or special shipments during transition.

G. Vendor relationships

1. Determine who are vendors to the source plant; local, national, international. Quantify terms of and prices for each contract. For bill of material components; supplies and service contracts for facility, warehousing, administration, maintenance; shipping materials, sales and marketing literature.

2. Establish extent of commitments to each vendor, and from each vendor.

3. Establish which vendors will be retained, and which will be shifted during the transition.

4. Cancel appropriate contracts. Replace them with others.

5. Revise contracts, changing addresses and delivery terms. Establish delivery timing and location during transition.

6. Set up new utility vendors as necessary, including power, water, gas, waste disposal, local and cell telephone, internet access.

7. Set up new transportation contracts, in and out.

8. Buy stationery, forms, etc. with new address, phone, fax.

◆ ◆ ◆

H. Day to day operation of a newly integrated facility

1. Separate or integrated departments for current and relocated operations.

2. Use / disposition of current and relocated equipment.

3. Sharing of common areas and facilities; e. g. docks.

4. Sharing transportation, e. g. a trucking company or U. P. S.

5. Sharing supervision and administration

6. Full time / part time; permanent or temporary employees.

7. Shifting workers between the existing and relocated operations

8. Same / different job descriptions, job grades, pay rates

9. Operator bidding between departments

10. Same / different quality standards between products

11. How to establish product priority when there are conflicts, assign limited resources

◆ ◆ ◆

I. Status of destination facility

1. Physical characteristics of facility and grounds, capacities and limitations: dimensions, shape, condition; floor, dock, elevators, heights, weight limits.

2. Space in manufacturing and process, storage, support, and administrative areas.

3. Incoming utility, communications and service capacities, discharges, environmental risks and permits required; capability for expansion.

4. Roads access and weight limits, parking, grounds.

◆ ◆ ◆

J. Plan for relocation and integration:

1. Process related
   a. Exactly what equipment is to be relocated? Until you have the exact list any layout is premature and will have to be changed. At the source facilities, technical characteristics will affect ability to be relocated and integrated, such as dependence on local technology and support, complexity, similarity to the destination.

   b. Documentation for process and technology: Procedures, training manuals, operator instructions, quality standards, inspection criteria. Set up instructions, maintenance manuals, preventive maintenance, equipment history, replacement parts stocked.

c. Process flow, plant layouts. Capacity of production equipment. Capability of equipment to produce different product models and styles. Capacity of materials handling and storage facilities and equipment. Environmental risks from past processes; presence of asbestos, PCB, lead, other hazards.

d. Manning and crew sizes, equipment, nominal and actual output and productivity, standard labor cost.

2. Inventory
What materials are to be relocated, sold, scrapped. Product related raw material, work in process, finished goods. Supplies for production, warehousing, administration, maintenance. Shippable materials; sales and marketing literature

3. Administrative and support
Equipment, furniture, fixtures to be relocated.

♦ ♦ ♦

K. Prepare the destination facility

1. Configure the destination facility based on what will go into it from the sources and the expansion planned. Get approvals. Mark services on the print. (Assumes that an existing facility will be used; if not, find and acquire an appropriate one.)

2. Modify or construct as needed. Walls, partitions, services, drains. Environmental permits, fire protection. Property zoning, easements, limitations. Permits required for addition or modification. Foreign Trade Zone, Enterprise zone, other community or state incentives.

3. Add operators and train them. Anticipate the production volumes and the headcount required for all functions. Retain trainers. Establish work methods, set up lesson plans, audio-visual assists, and training locations. If startup will be in parallel, set up preliminary equipment, tools and fixtures for training and first production. Get samples of parts and components. Establish expectations for operators and monitoring techniques. Hire people. permanent or temporary, in time to train them to adequate levels. Commence training and monitor operators.

4. Obtain adequate support in the destination community. At the source, determine the kinds of support necessary from suppliers and service providers. At the destination, locate companies who will provide the material or service either in the community or elsewhere.

L. Complete the relocation itself

1. Locate items to be moved on prints, mark them physically, put them on a list. Include manufacturing, process, maintenance, warehousing, receiving and shipping, support, administrative.

2. Obtain quotes for rigging, packing, moving and reinstallation services at source and destination.

3. Let contracts.

4. Monitor the execution of contracts.

5. Clean up the source plant according to contract.

6. Move in to the destination. Place all moved items in the appropriate locations.

♦ ♦ ♦

M. Start up the relocated equipment with the trained operators.

♦ ♦ ♦

Chapter 44   Typical sequence of actions, for a facility project

All facility projects are similar, and they are all different. These functions tend to be much the same in projects of all types.

A. First, concept stage for your circumstances

Project scope and timing
Preliminary justification
Geographic area guidance
Define interruption to business
H. R. ramifications and plan
Definition of facility, initial
Appoint project team
Disposal of source facility

◆ ◆ ◆

B. Site search if necessary

Define requirements for candidate communities, rank
Long list of communities
Short list of communities
Long list of possible sites
Short list of possible sites
Final facility choice
Mission of destination, final
Block plant layout
Acquisition
Recognize potential delay

◆ ◆ ◆

C. Layout of manufacturing, storage, offices

Detailed plant layout
Processes
New processes, equipment
Material in and out
Material storage and flow

Personnel flow
Computer, communications
To be moved
To be replaced, acquired
Docks, parking, grounds
Offices, support
Employee amenities

◆ ◆ ◆

D. Destination Construction

Prepare final specs
Construction or modification

◆ ◆ ◆

E. Transition Plan

Any changes in basic materials plan, batches, orders
Phasing of equipment move
Parallel operation required
H. R. actions detail
Let bids, rig and move
Award rig, move contracts
Computer transition
Communications transition
Security arrangements
Materials vendor changes?
Shipping changes?
Building service vendors?

◆ ◆ ◆

F. Preparation for move

Mark floor locations at destination
Accumulate documentation
Computer wiring plan
Communications wiring plan

Wire computer connections, telephones
Parallel operation, computer
Parallel operation, communications
Detail layout, stores, shops
Acquire materials handling
Mark objects to be moved
Pre-pack files, support
Security plan for move day
Detailed from / to charts for all gear to be moved

♦ ♦ ♦

G. Move day (days)

Pack documentation and records
Pack light cartons
Unplug, disconnect
Rig heavy equipment, move
Move equipment, furnishings
Move inventory
Security for the move

♦ ♦ ♦

H. Unpack, set up

Place heavy equipment
Place equipment, furnishings, associate documentation
Plug in, connect
Unpack light cartons
Place inventory
Change address, records

♦ ♦ ♦

I. Close up source facility

Dispose excess items
Clean up
Environmental clean up

Dispose of property

♦ ♦ ♦

J. Company mechanisms that increase ease and speed of project

Regulatory documentation exists throughout the organization; e. g. GMP, or ISO
Integrated computer information, ERP, MRP,
Product parts list, routers; computerized or manual
Plant and equipment layout on CAD - CAM
Plant utilities layout on CAD - CAM
Formal preventive maintenance program
Project management system

♦ ♦ ♦

Chapter 45   Made in (the name of your country here)

Discussion of the country of origin for manufactured products can easily deteriorate into emotional discourses on touchy subjects such as patriotism, protectionism, national pride. This chapter will try to avoid these pitfalls, and concentrate objectively on the practical and cost issues that will apply to your product, and whether it should be manufactured in your country, or elsewhere.

"Let the data drive the decision." When you run the numbers, you will have an objective idea of the cost magnitude involved; what you may gain or leave on the table.

Today, supply chain is a major concept, within the global perspective of facilities planning, and many people are working to smooth out the flow of goods through the supply chain. I'll suggest that in many cases, this work is waste, caused by indiscriminant and illogical pursuit of "cheap goods". Make them at home (wherever your home is) and avoid costs in several different categories, delay, miscommunication, transportation, long lead times, obsolescence. Make them at home and pull many no-longer-necessary tasks out of supply chain administration, cut travel and communications budgets, as well as finance and legal cost. Slice the likelihood of product recall and negative publicity.

In support of this point, remember that Taichi Ohno said in quite clear terms that inventory is 'waste'. In Lean Six Sigma a major objective is the elimination of the seven kinds of wastes, of which Transportation, Inventory, and Defects are well represented in international mass production.

Do you remember recalls due to lead paint, adulterated milk, contaminated food? Local economies put out of action by bird flu strains, SARS, recently MERS-CoV, by popular uprisings or terrorism, by a tsunami? Collapsing buildings where products were manufactured for export?

Floods, tornados, hurricanes, earthquakes, can happen anywhere, and the supply chain is not able to forecast and avoid these disasters. Their real cost after all is measured in lives, and destruction, not just the late shipment of a container of the latest athletic shoe or cell phone.

As in all sourcing decisions, there are many site sensitive costs involved. While offshore labor rates may be much less, most other incremental costs will be greater. And today, one of those skyrocketing costs is energy, to ship the goods to market.

Please consider the following questions, all to answer the basis question, what will be the cost difference. You may not get this guidance from major consulting groups at all.

◆ ◆ ◆

A. Labor

For many manufacturers, loaded direct labor cost is typically less than 10% of the cost of goods sold. In one of the most extreme differentials today, South East Asia labor is one-fifth the U. S. cost, which translates to a maximum difference of 8% of the cost of goods sold. And that difference is decreasing as Asian labor rates climb, sometimes steeply.

But that's not the only consideration, even for the labor portion of the comparison. For example what is the cost of benefits to workers? Are there mandated holidays, housing, meals, transportation and 13th month benefits costs to take into account?

Next, consider the two types of labor variance, price and usage. Although your labor price will almost certainly go down, what about the usage variation and hours worked? If labor rate is half as much, and productivity is 50% compared to on-shore, that's a net wash.

◆ ◆ ◆

B. Equipment / Facilities

What will you do about equipment? If it is available offshore, add acquisition and startup costs and perhaps a write-down in the home country. Otherwise, pay to move or buy, and equipment is often taxed as it is imported.

Next, throw in the maintenance cost charge (how well will equipment be maintained; how much down time can be anticipated?)

Next, ask what the learning curve might be like for an offshore facility with respect to labor and material losses as it approaches a steady state.

Finally, what will the steady state output be? What about utilization, efficiency, productivity, material usage? Don't forget direct to indirect labor factors, expatriate workers and their costs, turnover rates, theft and security.

◆ ◆ ◆

C. Materials

Materials tend to be priced at a worldwide level, and so may not vary significantly. Be sure to factor in import duties. Confirm local product pricing.

D. Shipping Freight

Freight, insurance, product damage, obsolescence, tariffs, and brokers fees all contribute to the cost of the landed product. But today, the cost of fuel to ship the goods is the predominant factor. News reports continue, something like "As the cost of shipping continues to soar along with fuel prices, homegrown manufacturing jobs are making a comeback after decades of decline. While it once cost $3,000 to ship a container halfway around the world, it now costs $8,000, prompting some businesses to look closer to home for manufacturing needs."

◆ ◆ ◆

E. Product recalls

Regulation within individual countries is frequently the target of criticism. However, that regulation often forbids the use of unauthorized materials; melamine, lead based paints and industrial grade chemicals in food products, and outlawed antibiotics for instance. People are paid a higher wage in developed countries, but the manufacturing climate can more than justify that wage rate because products recalls are much less frequent. When a company has no products on the market, and lawsuits are filed because of customer injury, wage rate savings are quickly lost.

◆ ◆ ◆

F. Health Issues

Health issues seem to continue to occur in some areas of the world, for instance bird flu strains, SARS, recently MERS-CoV. When these issues arise, workers are affected, plants are shut, production in stopped, and shipments held up.

Suppliers are sometimes accused of safety and child labor abuse, the suicide rate may be high in plants, and exports suffer accordingly.

Our crystal ball is not clear enough to predict when and where in the world the next major health issue will arise, and the overall impact may well be much greater than missed shipments. But history of the first part of the 21st century indicates that developed countries will not be the center of the problem.

◆ ◆ ◆

G. Local operations

How will operations in your home country change? Will you incur costs to phase out a local facility?

Plant admin at home will have to be eliminated at a cost, if the product is moved offshore, and admin added and trained there. Will the tricks of the trade be relocated?

◆ ◆ ◆

H. Travel for support

Consider higher executive and technician travel to support the offshore location as well as special mail and priority shipments of documents, models, specs and products. Modern communications technology can only do so much to mitigate distance, language barriers and the lack of face to face meetings.

Who in the organization will perform product design, new product development and engineering; what about the model shop and pilot plant? Remember, too, that new product transition is problematic even when headquarters is in the building next door.

Who will perform Human Relations oversight? Who will exercise quality oversight and how? What about procurement? Will you see the product and its components for the first time when the product is in the stores or your warehouse? Who will provide financial oversight within the new company? How about independent auditing? Although auditors in developed countries hardly have a pristine record, they do function under a (more or less) transparent regulatory regime.

◆ ◆ ◆

I. The cycle time

Can you practice Just in Time with product on the high seas, subject to typhoons and port work stoppage? Have you planned additional inventory to cover transportation lead times? With extended inventories, will scrap and obsolescence costs increase?

How will your Time-To-Market change? Local manufacture offers the shortest time-to-market, from product design to prototype to test run to manufacture to ship to customer, especially considering reaction times to changes inherent in the process. For some companies, such as those in the apparel and fashion business, time-to-market is the deciding factor.

In any business, the advantages of vertical integration, cycle time, lower shipping costs and the ability to advertise "sweatshop free" were decisive in convincing them to continue manufacturing locally.

As a result of long cycle times and transportation, will products be obsolescent or damaged by the time they arrive?

♦ ♦ ♦

J. Made in (name of your country)

What is the label "Made in the (name of your country)" worth to your company and to good will? Does the label imply quality, to your benefit?

And here is the place, in this discourse, to consider those emotional, touchy subjects such as patriotism, protectionism, national pride, and how they will affect your national sales.

♦ ♦ ♦

K. Off shore legal and political considerations.

Will practices and laws in the new country limit executive actions? Can you eliminate jobs in the future? At what cost? This question by the way is appropriate not just in emerging countries.

How will you establish and defend your real and intellectual property rights? Is foreign ownership possible? Are you ready to partner with a local entity? Remember, disputes will most likely be adjudicated in the country of implantation. Is the local banking system healthy and vigorous? Is the legal system friendly to investors? Review the various national rankings, for topics such as graft and corruption.

♦ ♦ ♦

L. Tax and accounting issues

Consider the political vagaries of local tax law. What happens if the deduction of expenses to transfer jobs offshore is disallowed? Can you continue your business strategy?
What are profit repatriation tax rules in both the host and local country? Whose rules will apply to inter-company accounts such as transfer pricing?

◆ ◆ ◆

M. Foreign exchange

Are you ready and able to predict accurately and respond effectively to fluctuations in exchange rates that affect raw materials and operations? Do you plan to use common currency hedging strategies to minimize exposure?

◆ ◆ ◆

N. Local codes and local cultures

Countries around the world are different, and traveling in them is all the more enjoyable for it. But doing business in different cultures can bring out inefficiencies. Local practices and business codes are not necessarily wrong by any means. Residents who are used to them may judge that the standards imposed on them, from afar, are confusing and irrational.

Inefficiency arises when differences in codes, culture, practices are identified and reconciled. Gee, we don't do it that way; please explain to me just what you want; we'll have to figure out how to do it that way; it may actually clash with this practice of ours; these materials are not easily available. If conflicting practices are not identified and reconciled the potential damage can be much worse. Heads up.

◆ ◆ ◆

Chapter 46   Examples of plant layout drawing

Principles of plant layout and design will apply to most industrial situations. The layout examples in this chapter encompass a wide variety of facility characteristics, and of process characteristics.

No example is likely to fit your exact needs, because building, dimensions, and process vary so much. Utilize these examples together with basic principles, found in this book, or in Jack Greene's <u>Industrial Engineering: Theory, Practice & Application.</u>

<u>Index of sample drawings</u>

<u>A. Single story building</u>
1. Straight line flow
2. U shaped flow
3. In a building designed for distribution, adapt to another use
4. To place permanent equipment and avoid later interference
5. Distribution center
6. Cellular flow
7. Modular work flow
8. Clean room for sterile or aseptic liquids
9. Clean room for devices, semiconductors
10. Primary Conveyor, fed from other conveyors, from above
11. One product, with several components, not conveyorized
12. Cell and modular elements in the same layout
13. Electronics fab and test
14. Integrated plastics product
15. From dedicated cells into modular packaging lines
16. Model and prototype shops, pilot plant

<u>B. Multi-story building</u>
1. Multi-story building, utilize vertical flow
2. Multi-story building, two elevators
3. Multi-story building, one elevator
4. Multi-story building, services on another floor

<u>C. Buildings set on plot plans</u>
1. Outside storage, liquid and dry bulk materials

2. Outside storage, large components and product handling
3. Constrained by adjoining property
4. Unconstrained by adjoining property
5. Details of dock characteristics

See http://jacksonproductivity.com.draw.pdf for these same examples of plant layout and design within particular building types. On line they are easier to read and print out, and I am able to add to them.

♦ ♦ ♦

A   1   Straight Line Flow

Flow is essentially straight line, although it adapts to building design.

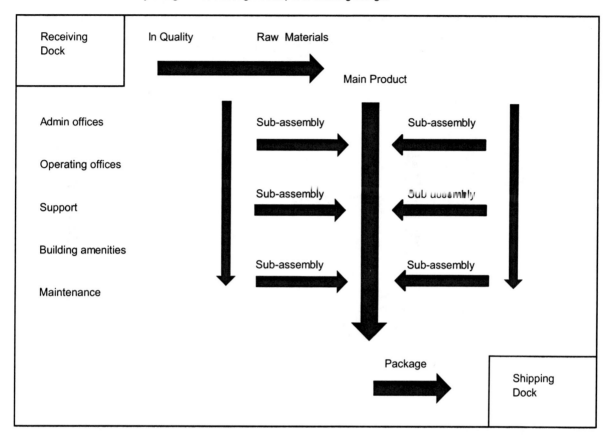

185

A   2   U Shaped Flow
In and out of the same dock

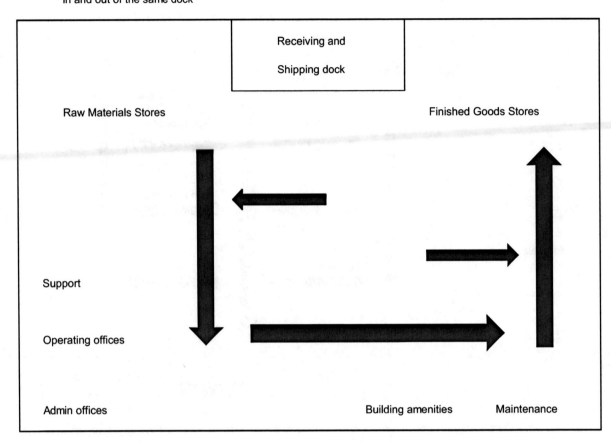

A 3 Example of a building designed for distribution, adapted to another use

Many of these facilities are empty and available. They are characterized by multiple docks and doors.
Take advantage of the docks to improve process flow for your operation. Close up the unused doors and docks.

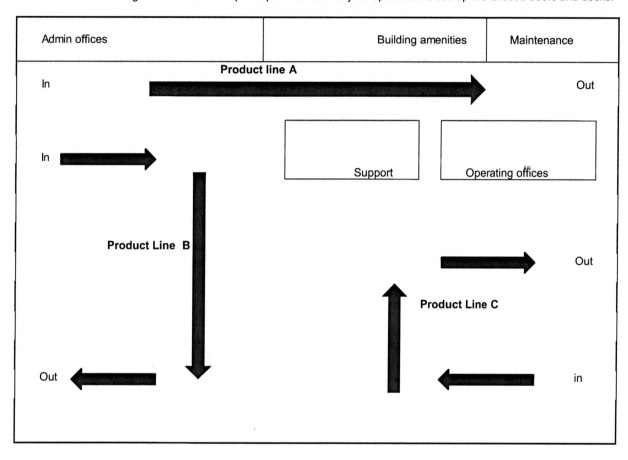

A 4 To place permanent equipment and avoid later interference

Position fixed, hard to relocate, functions and equipment along a wall that will not be used for later expansion. Place equipment outside as well as inside exterior walls. Later, expand along other walls.

Outside,	Inside,
Hoppers	Liquid waste disposal
Bins	Rest rooms
Tanks	Fire sprinkler risers
Solid waste	In power
Water tower	In gas
Dust collection	Water softening
	Water purification
Dumpster	Blow-out walls
Pallets	Plating, degreasing
	Motor control centers
	Process using mezzanine

A 5 Distribution center arrangement

A DC will have many docks, and many storage racks. Straight line or U-shaped flow will depend on dock location. Reduce travel by careful location of materials in racks; warehousing programs will help.

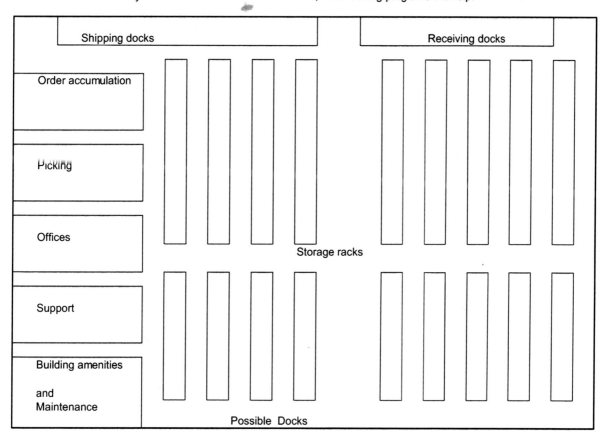

A   6   Cellular flow

An approach in which manufacturing work centers (cells) have the total capabilities needed to produce an item or group of similar items.

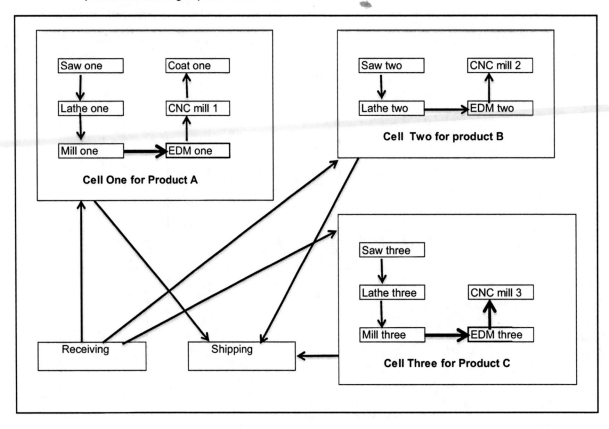

A   7   Modular work flow

Modular work centers consist of similar equipment or capabilities, and products move among multiple work centers before they are completed.   With or without conveyor lines.

Saw module for all products	Products A, B, C are routed to the module if work is to be performed there; on a dedicated or a multi-product machine. Different product, different flow.	Lathes module for all products
Mill module for all products		EDM module for all products
CNC mill module for all products		Coating module for all products

A   8   Clean room for sterile or aseptic liquids

Characterized by material pass thrus, employee change rooms, sterilization.
With or without conveyor lines.

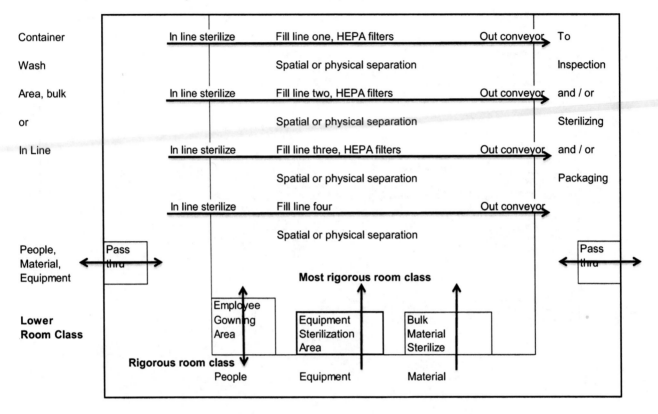

A   9   Clean room for devices, semiconductors
Characterized by material pass thrus, employee change rooms, superior HVAC
Usually involves conveyors

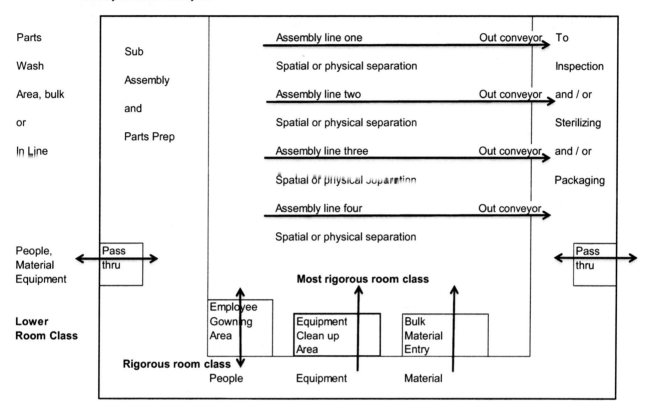

Parts

Wash

Area, bulk

or

In Line

Sub

Assembly

and

Parts Prep

Assembly line one   Out conveyor   To

Spatial or physical separation   Inspection

Assembly line two   Out conveyor   and / or

Spatial or physical separation   Sterilizing

Assembly line three   Out conveyor   and / or

Spatial or physical separation   Packaging

Assembly line four   Out conveyor

Spatial or physical separation

People,
Material
Equipment

Pass
thru

Pass
thru

**Lower
Room Class**

Most rigorous room class

Employee
Gowning
Area

Equipment
Clean up
Area

Bulk
Material
Entry

Rigorous room class

People   Equipment   Material

A 10   Primary Conveyor, fed from other conveyors, from above
Detail is driven by the product components and sequence of steps and assembly.

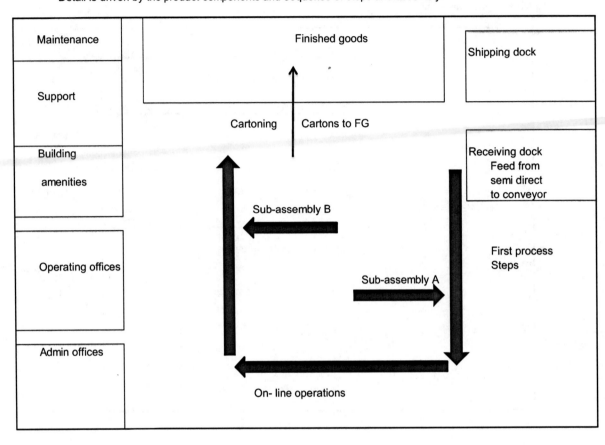

A 11 One product, with several components, not conveyorized

This example shows kitting, sub assemblies, final assembly, test, pack, ship in a U shape..

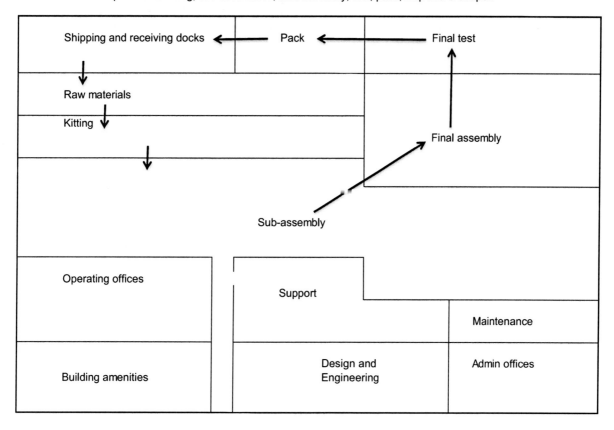

A 12   Cell and modular elements in the same layout
Not an uncommon arrangement, especially when equipment has accumulated over time.
With or without conveyor lines.

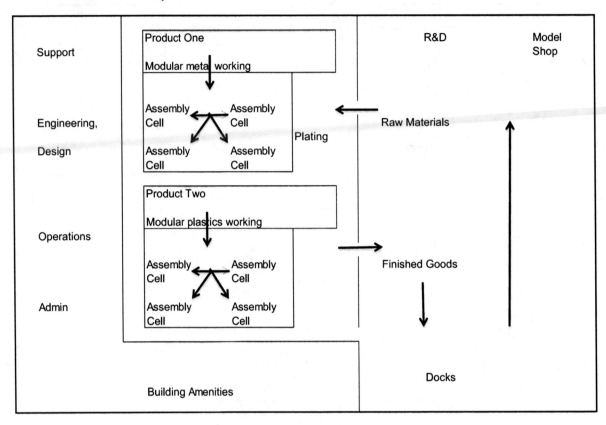

A 13   Electronics fab and test

Integrated manufacture; subassembly, fab, assembly, and test in clean rooms.
Because parts are small, materials handling moves many parts at one time.

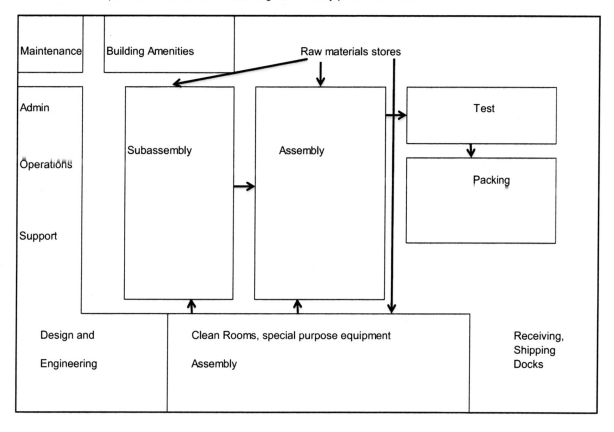

A 14   Integrated plastics product
Molding, sub-assembly, tumbling barrels for smoothing, assembly, through distribution

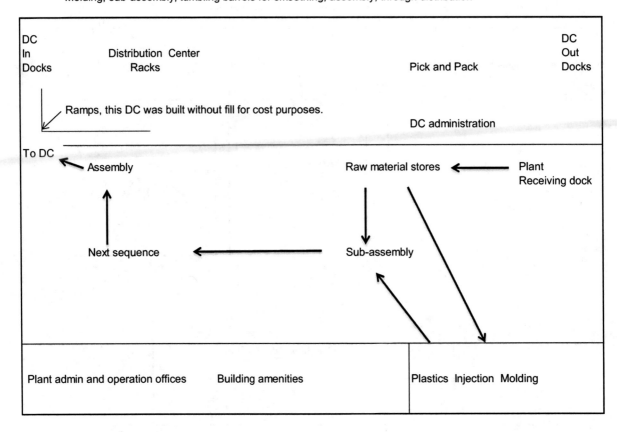

A 15   From dedicated cells into modular packaging lines

A typical layout; in this example specialized product filling flows into general purpose inspection and packing.

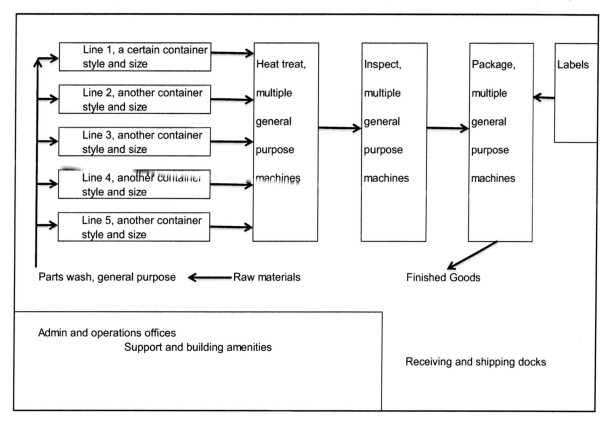

A 16   Model and prototype shops, pilot plant

These operations will have both specialized and general purpose machines. They will be called on to produce any product, with as little subcontracted as possible. If associated with production operations, these shops should be able to match or simulate all production equipment.

Specialty shops will depend on the charter of the organization, and may contain one or more of the following:

Metal working, classic	Wood working	Plumbing
Metal working, Cad Cam	Plastics working, layup	Hydraulics
Electrical	Composites working, layup	Instrumentation
Electronic	Welding	Fill
Sheet metal, cut and form	Plating	Package
Sandblast	Paint	Label
Chemistry	Multi-layer printing	Exact measurement
Assembly	Signs, printing	Optics

Design and engineering offices, Cad Cam equipment

Model and prototype shops are not the place for Just in Time material delivery, no matter what . the black belts say. The predictability of work, the horizon, is not clear enough to allow lead times.. Inventory should keep on hand a wide variety of materials, because the shop will be called on to produce and modify on short notice. Reliable local sources if any can allow a smaller inventory.

Layout of machines should concentrate on fitting them into the space with regard to safety and material handling, because the flow of materials will likely be unpredictable and irregular . If possible leave ample access space for material, and for new equipment and technology.

B   1   Multi-story building, utilize vertical flow

Where possible, utilize vertical flow to move product.

A practical handling system is necessary to place material on the upper floor to start.

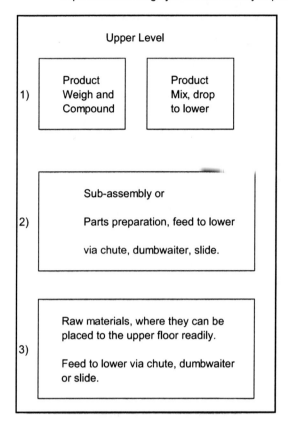

Upper Level

1) Product Weigh and Compound | Product Mix, drop to lower

2) Sub-assembly or

Parts preparation, feed to lower

via chute, dumbwaiter, slide.

3) Raw materials, where they can be placed to the upper floor readily.

Feed to lower via chute, dumbwaiter or slide.

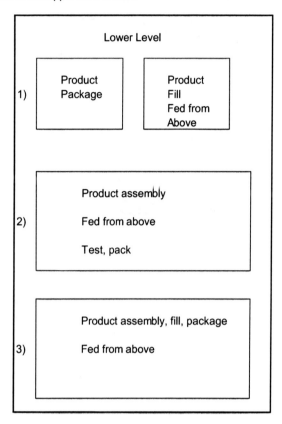

Lower Level

1) Product Package | Product Fill Fed from Above

2) Product assembly

Fed from above

Test, pack

3) Product assembly, fill, package

Fed from above

B 2   Multi-story building, two elevators

Except for the fact that material must use an elevator, flow can be productive.
Many options are possible.

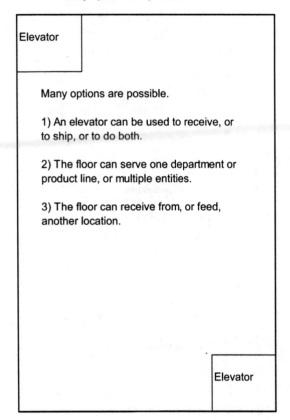

Many options are possible.

1) An elevator can be used to receive, or
to ship, or to do both.

2) The floor can serve one department or
product line, or multiple entities.

3) The floor can receive from, or feed,
another location.

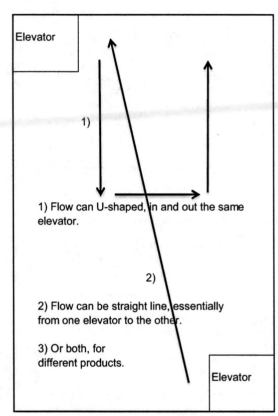

1) Flow can U-shaped, in and out the same
elevator.

2) Flow can be straight line, essentially
from one elevator to the other.

3) Or both, for
different products.

B   3   Multi-story building, one elevator

The area near the elevator will be busy, and should be kept open.
Careful layout will be useful to maintain productivity.

1) The elevator will be used to receive and ship.

2) Flow can only be U-shaped, in and out
of the same elevator, unless vertical feed .
is possible through chute, slide, or
dumbwaiter.

3) The floor can serve one department or
product line, or multiple entities. Use
will depend on size and ingenuity of
layout applied.

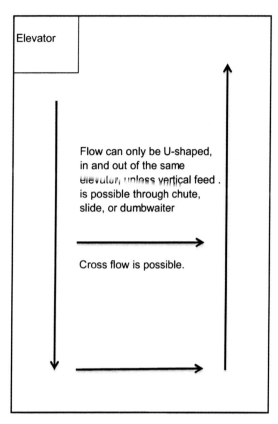

Flow can only be U-shaped,
in and out of the same
elevator, unless vertical feed .
is possible through chute,
slide, or dumbwaiter

Cross flow is possible.

B   4   Multi-story building, services on another floor

The operations floor can be effectively laid out because services and amenities are on another floor.
In this example, services are located on only a partial floor, under manufacturing.

Upper Level, Operations

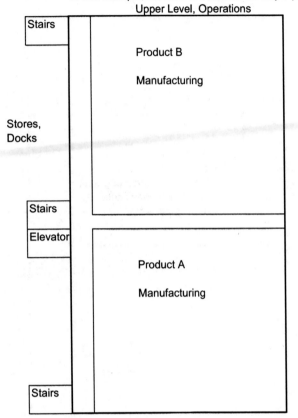

Lower Level

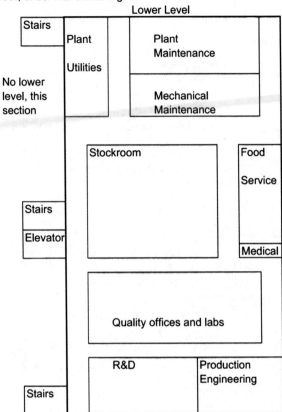

C   1   Outside storage, liquid and dry bulk materials

Outside storage is often practical. Outside containers do not take up plant space, and they can be filled by truck easily.

Be sure that permanent containers do not block future plant expansion

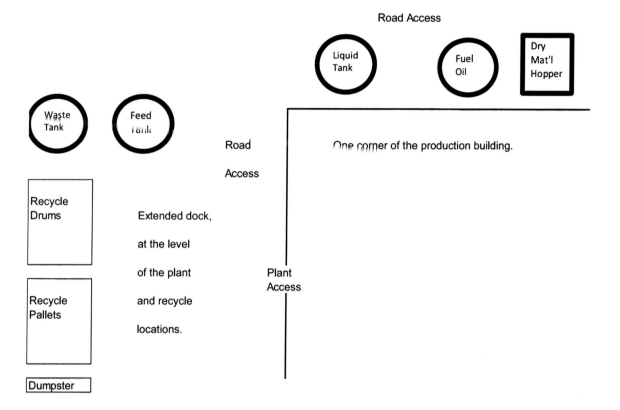

Road Access

Liquid Tank

Fuel Oil

Dry Mat'l Hopper

Waste Tank

Feed Tank

Road

Access

Recycle Drums

Recycle Pallets

Dumpster

Extended dock,

at the level

of the plant

and recycle

locations.

Plant Access

One corner of the production building.

C 2 Outside storage, large components and product handling

Large weather-proof components sometimes can be kept outside.
Be sure that permanent containers do not block future plant expansion

Horizontal racks for long components

One corner of the production building.

Horizontal storage of tall sections

Temporary trailer

C 3   Constrained by adjoining property

Placement of permanent equipment is key when building expansion is blocked in some directions. Locate permanent equipment along the sides that are already blocked.

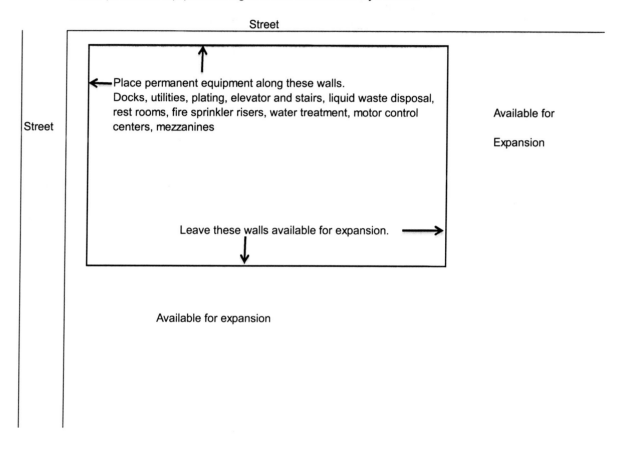

C 4 Unconstrained by adjoining property

Placement of permanent equipment is key when building expansion is blocked in some directions. Locate permanent equipment along the sides that are already blocked.

Available for expansion

Available for

Expansion

Initial building
Place permanent equipment along no more than two walls, or centrally.

Probably locate docks first considering street access, grade levels, appearance, and distances. Then plan interior layouts accordingly.

Available for

Expansion

Available for expansion

CPSIA information can be obtained at www.ICGtesting.com
Printed in the USA
LVOW09s0704120716

495875LV00006BA/387/P